STRONG TEENS
strong Neighborhoods
Teens write about friends, family and community

Edited by Youth Communication

Editors
Loretta Chan
Al Desetta
Keith Hefner

YOUTH
COMMUNICATION
True Stories by Teens

STRONG TEENS
strOng NeighbOrhOods

Contributing Editors
Rachel Blustain, Al Desetta, Andrea Estepa, Katia Hetter,
Phil Kay, Carol Kelly, Nora McCarthy, Tamar Rothenberg,
Robin Shulman and Hope Vanderberg.

Layout & Design
Jeff Faerber and Efrain Reyes

Cover Art
Patricia Battles

ISBN 978-1-933939-69-8

Second Edition
Printed in the United States of America

Youth Communication
224 West 29th St. - 2nd fl.
New York, NY 10001
www.youthcomm.org

To the teens of New York City

TABLE OF CONTENTS

Contents

Contents

Making It, Making a Difference

FAMILY, FRIENDS AND ME

CAN'T AFFORD TO FOLLOW: MY FAMILY IS TOO IMPORTANT TO ME

By Charlene George

I heard the same things from my new friends at middle school nearly every day. "Yo, Charlene, let's not go to school today. Let's go smoke and get some alcohol. Let's maybe go to the movies, museum or the zoo, but let's not go to school today." They seemed really nice, and when they spoke about all the fun places they went during school, I decided to join them. I wanted to hang out with them and be the type of friend they said was cool.

One day we went to the movie theater and saw five movies—but we only paid for one. It was so great to see action, funny and scary movies that had just come out, all in one day. Then my friends told me to steal $20 from my mom so we could go to the movies again. They also wanted me to buy some things for them. I didn't want to let them down, so I said OK. But I couldn't bring myself to steal from my mom. Instead, I pretended that I'd stolen from her, when I really had $20 saved up.

I lived with my foster mom, and I'd been with her since I was 7 years old. I felt she really wanted the best for me. I wondered why my friends never wanted to talk about their own families, and why none of them could say even one good thing about their parents.

But I kept on doing things with my friends to show that I was one of them. About three weeks after I started cutting school with them, we went to the Bay Plaza mall. We didn't have any money, so we were just window-shopping and looking around in a store called "Rainbow."

Then, to my surprise, my mother's good friend Kim popped out of the back. It turned out that she worked there. She asked me what I was doing there during school hours.

Before I could answer, the man who worked at the counter started yelling at my friends. It wasn't a pretty sight the way he was grabbing them, like his nails were digging into their skin. Their bodies were leaning to the side and they were screaming, "Help, he's hurting me!"

When the boss went over to the counter to see what was going on, I was shocked. My friends were stealing small items like candy, earrings and fake rings that would turn your fingers green in a second. He called the police and my friends looked afraid, like they were wondering where their lives were headed now.

When the police came, they needed my friends' family information so their parents could come get them. Most of them had their parents come to pick them up. But when the police asked the two ringleaders of our group about their families, their faces looked shocked, like the time we all cut school to see scary movies. The two ringleaders said they didn't have any information to give the police. For the first time, I suspected that they didn't have anyone taking care of them to come pick them up. The policemen took them to the station, and I never heard from them again.

> **I thought to myself that my future couldn't be a jail cell. It had to be a home and family.**

As they left the store, it hit me that maybe they cut school and stole things because they had no one taking care of them and teaching them how to act. But I did, so why was I acting this way? I imagined being locked up away from my mother, just because I wanted to be a follower. I thought to myself that my future couldn't be a jail cell. It had to be a home and family.

I was lucky to have my foster mother and I didn't want to lose her. I asked myself, "Am I going to let this peer pressure keep getting to me?" Doing what they asked me to do was only getting me in trouble.

Luckily, while my friends were stealing, I was standing next to Kim. After the police left, Kim made sure that I went home right away. She said she knew that I wasn't the type to steal. She said, "I'm not

going to tell your mom," and that made me feel really happy.

Then she said, "You have to tell her all by yourself. Letting your mom know would show her what you did wrong, but it would also show that you're growing up." I was upset. I'd hoped that Kim would let me go without telling anyone. But I knew I had to tell my mother, because sooner or later the truth would probably come out.

When I got home, I told my mother how I'd cut school that day. Her face got really crazy and her eyes were almost poking out of her head. As she yelled at me, she was spitting so much that my sister was wiping off her face like it was raining cats and dogs. "You are grounded for one whole week with no TV and no electronics," my mother said. "I'll be coming up to your room to take the phone away from you."

An hour later, my mother had calmed down. We started talking about the issue all over again. She told me I still had to do my punishment so I'd learn from my mistakes, but that she was happy I'd told her all by myself. (She didn't know Kim had made me tell her.)

That's when I realized that Kim really helped me by making me start doing things on my own. Even though she didn't know me that well, she helped make me choose whether or not I wanted to keep giving in to peer pressure.

I realized that when I want to change, my friends, Kim or my mother can't make that change for me—I have to stop smoking, drinking and hanging out with my old friends. For one whole week, I hung out by myself. Now that I was going to school every day, I didn't see my old friends because they were still cutting. After school I'd go home and watch the Disney Channel, Law and Order and CSI during my free time. I was being a good person, but I got really bored and lonely.

I felt like I was walking through a maze trying to find some new friends. Then, after a week and a half, I met a boy named Peter and girl named Vicky at a swim meet after school. They both went to my school and were in my swim group.

I started going to their houses to play video games and chilling

with them at the movie theater. One time, the three of us had a conversation about being able to tell each other the truth. Even though it felt a little funny saying it, we all admitted that we had cheated on tests before. We knew cheating was wrong, but we all felt good that we shared something with each other.

Peter and Vicky didn't pressure me to skip school, drink or smoke. We didn't hang out on the street getting in trouble. I was still going to school, earning good grades and perfect attendance and putting a smile on my mother's face.

When we went to the movies, I remembered my old friends sitting next to me. I remembered jumping because we were scared of the movie, with the popcorn going up into the air and getting on the people in front of us—and them thinking we threw it at them. Those were the good old days. But if I were still listening to my old friends, I would be just like a remote control car, going everywhere they wanted, and just being used all the time.

Recently, one of my classmates asked me to slap another classmate on the back of the head when he was asleep, so no one would know who did it. I told him that if he was so big and bad, he should do it himself. Now when I get pressure from a peer, I deal with it by using my brain. I go back to my memory of when I messed up with my old friends, and I tell myself I don't want to face those consequences again.

THE CREW FROM THE PARKING LOT

By Ferentz Lafargue

The parking lot behind Wertheimer's department store on Jamaica Avenue was once a place where a lot of boyhood dreams were born. Dreams of growing up and playing for the Yankees or Giants someday, dreams of meeting that girl, the one you knew was out there, the one that was made for you. My friends and I used to spend the whole afternoon there playing baseball, football, manhunt, and practically anything else you could think of.

One day we noticed a piece of wood in the corner of the lot. We found a rock to prop it up and made ourselves a bicycle ramp. We practiced jumping for a week or two until the wood broke and it was back to playing bike tag and waiting for the next thing to come along.

Every winter when it snowed, there would be huge piles of snow in the corners of the lot. We would start out by doing some light skiing to get warmed up and soften up the snow. (The skis were made of the finest cardboard we could find.) But we all know what happens when you put a bunch of guys somewhere with snow...Snowfight!

The rules were simple: whichever mountain you were on was your territory and whoever was with you was your team. We would fight until one team captured the other team's mountain or the teams split up and everyone started fighting amongst themselves. When that happened it was every man for himself. We would go home looking like we had just climbed Mt. Everest and sometimes I think that would have been easier.

We also shared a lot of disappointments in the parking lot. We felt bad for Ed when he didn't make the varsity basketball team. We felt

---

(Note: The names in this story have been changed.)

sorry when Devon's girl Wendy moved away. (They were the royal couple of the parking lot.) When Abner and Carlos were sent to fight in the Persian Gulf War we all kept an eye on the news. There weren't any me's or I's in the parking lot—we were a team.

But these days the parking lot is just used for parking cars. We don't even keep in touch like we used to. Rarely will you see two of us together. Some have moved away, the rest just feel like they're miles away. At least to me they do. The only thing we all have in common is that we grew up.

When I look around now and see people that I used to be down with back in the days, I feel really sorry for some of these guys.

Devon was the superstar of the parking lot. He could throw, run, catch—the whole nine. We used to think he was the total package. We thought he would play high school baseball or football, then get drafted or get a scholarship, and go on to become a major leaguer. But instead of going out for one of the teams, he opted to be down with the fellas, hanging out and doing things like robbing people, stealing chains, or getting caught up in stupid gang battles.

> **When I look around now and see people that I used to be down with back in the days, I feel really sorry for some of these guys.**

Now he's one of the people who comes up to me and talks about how he messed up, how he should have stayed in school. Now the only things he strives for are his own apartment, a G.E.D., a job, and a car. Devon's only 18 and has been sent to Riker's Island Jail two times already. The sad thing is he has no fear of going back.

Devon's younger brother John was a pretty good ballplayer too but more importantly he was a B+ student and a born leader. He was never afraid of being team captain. In fact, he thrived on it. He used to talk about joining the Marines and getting his M-14. Now John is 17 and has a kid and he's not even close to a high school diploma. He was hardly ever in school last year. The word is that John is dealing guns. An M-14 is probably child's play compared to some of the guns he's come in contact with.

Then there's Angel. Angel used to be my best friend and in a way he always will be. Angel had drive and determination. One summer he lost his glove and, being that he was the only lefty in the parking lot, he had no one to lend him one. But Angel decided not to let that keep him on the sidelines. He found a right-handed glove and for about a year and a half he tried to be right-handed. He started doing almost everything right-handed.

Eventually he got another left-handed glove. But even after that you could occasionally see him tricking an opposing batter with a wicked right-handed curve ball. Angel hasn't dropped out yet, not officially, but I doubt he goes to school more than five full days a year. When he does go he usually cuts out early in the day. Now Angel's dealing drugs. He used to have determination but these days the only thing he seems determined to do is mess up his life

The sad thing is that these are the guys that little kids look up to. The other day me and one of my friends were walking down 89th Avenue and one of my little brother's friends came up to us with a fake blunt that he had rolled up, and was telling us how good it was. This kid is 10 years old at most. But you really can't blame him. That's what he sees around him. That's what's considered cool.

The ones that plan to go on to college go so that as soon as they're finished and have some money in the bank, they can move as far away from the neighborhood as fast as they can. My homeboy Abner, for example, hasn't even graduated from college yet and he's already beginning the process. He recently moved to Forest Hills and if it weren't for his parents you'd never see his face around the block at all.

He even started to forget people's names. There's one girl he's known for about 10 or 15 years now and the other day he couldn't come up with her name. It made me wonder if he remembers mine.

Then there's me. I was the youngest kid in the parking lot, which meant I was last to get picked for the teams and the first to get picked on. I was like everyone's little brother. I never made it to the forefront; I just stood back and watched everyone else. I looked up to these guys.

But I knew the real them. I was smart enough to learn from their mistakes.

They still keep an eye out for me. Every time one of them sees one of my articles or hears about me doing anything else good, he's always ready to congratulate me and tell me to keep it up. It's almost like I'm their last hope of success: if I come out OK then they'll honestly be able to say they had a hand in raising me.

I intend to go to college and study communications and advertising. Hopefully one day I'll be writing for a big-time newspaper or working for an advertising company. Then I'd like to make sure my little brother gets his act together, help fix up my neighborhood, and do whatever I can to help out some of my old friends. But whatever I end up doing, one thing I won't do is let those guys down and mess up my life.

While writing this article I discovered that I'm a pretty lucky guy after all. Remembering all those good times we had in the parking lot was enough to make me cry. I hope everyone has a parking lot in their lives. What good is a tree without its roots?

LOSING MY FRIENDS TO WEED

By Jamel Salter

I had a lot of friends in East Flatbush, Brooklyn who I grew up with. Growing up together made us very close—until my friends got too close to weed. Before that happened, we were always together. We'd go to movies, parties, the park, and if we didn't have anywhere to go, we'd stay at one of our houses and play video games.

Even though we were close friends, we still had our little arguments. But when we argued, Dave would get in the middle and try to stop it. He was like the official peacemaker of the group. Dave had the best sense of humor out of all of us. He was always telling jokes. That was one of the best things about hanging with them, you always got a good laugh.

But one day, when my friends were about 14, they made plans to put money in to buy some weed. I didn't want to put any money in because I didn't want to have anything to do with weed. I thought if I didn't put any money in they would say I couldn't smoke and I would pretend I was disappointed. But they got enough money to go through with it and said I could smoke anyway.

Someone had to ride his bike to go get it. I live on 54th and the closest place to buy is on 19th, so he had to ride 35 blocks. (The things people do for drugs!!)

We were at the park when they started smoking it. One person lit the blunt, took a puff, and passed it around. I was in total shock because I had read and seen about drugs on television and here it was right in front of me. As it was going around I was thinking to myself, "What should I do? Should I say yes or no?" I looked at how my friends were reacting after they smoked it. Since it was their first time, everyone coughed hard after they took a puff.

I sat at the end of the line, hoping that they would finish the blunt

before it got to me or that someone else would turn it down so that I wouldn't be the only one who refused. Neither happened, and I found myself being handed the blunt. "Chill yo, I don't want any."

"Take a puff son, it's mad nice."

"If you don't smoke, you're a herb."

"You can't be a mama's boy the rest of your life."

I got so tempted that I actually took it in my hand. But I knew that it was a choice between smoking and keeping their friendship or not smoking and keeping my health. I came to my senses and just passed it on.

"You really are a herb."

"You can't hang, mama's boy."

When they finished smoking, they started acting like fools. They were hitting each other and cracking stupid jokes. Seeing the way they acted made me glad that I didn't smoke. The next day everyone was talking about how bad they felt in the morning. You would think that would make them come to their senses and stop, but they just started making plans to get more.

> **It was a choice between smoking and keeping their friendship or not smoking and keeping my health.**

My friends have been smoking for a year now and it has changed them. They always look like zombies. Their eyes are always red and halfway closed. They have bad tempers and they are always ready to fight. Especially Dave, now he has the baddest temper of all them all.

A few weeks ago we were at the park playing basketball. Dave had the ball and when I tried to steal it from him, I slapped his hand by accident. He got highly upset and started yelling at me. "Why the hell are you fouling me?"

"It was an accident, and I don't know what you're getting mad about anyway," I told him. "It's all a part of the game. If you can't deal with it, don't play."

Dave tried to punch me but missed, then the others held him back and calmed him down. This surprised me because Dave was always

the peacemaker before he began to smoke pot.

My friends and I always used to play against other blocks in bas-ketball, and I always started. I didn't hear about a game for a while but I didn't worry, because I figured my friends would tell me when they were playing. Then one day I called Dave to see what he was doing and his mother picked up.

"Hello, this is Jamel. Is Dave there?"

"No, he isn't, Jamel. He went to the park about a half-hour ago."

When I got to the park I saw them just finishing playing the 51st Street team. I got upset because I always started and now, because I don't smoke weed, they didn't even bother to call me. (By the way, they lost.)

Not being close to my friends like I used to be makes me think to myself, "Maybe I should smoke it just one time. What's the worst thing that could happen to me?" Then I remember the way that they were acting the other day in the park and I just forget about it.

You might be wondering why I don't stop trying to stay close to them and make new friends, but it isn't so easy to lose friends you've grown up with. I keep trying to talk them out of smoking, because I don't want that stuff to make them sick. But they just laugh as if I'm stupid and tell me to mind my own business.

I wish our friendship could go back to the way it was before, but I don't think there's any chance of that happening while they keep smoking. I used to think that they were true friends, but now I know that it was just a game. If not smoking is the reason why I've lost my friends, then I've been cheated. It's hard to believe that the difference between friends or no friends comes from one little blunt.

WHY IS YOUR BEST FRIEND YOUR BEST FRIEND?

By Tina Li

No, she did not run into a burning building or stand in front of a speeding bullet to save my life, but what she does makes her every bit as valuable to me as a best friend.

Just by her being there, I have found a confidante, a person to share joys and sorrows with, a person to have fun with, and just to talk to and be close to. She's one of the most sympathetic and understanding people I know and I don't know of anyone who is as willing as she is to share in my burdens.

In junior high, when my other friends used to tease me, she would come to my defense when my feelings were hurt. When this bully used to pull my hair, she would step in and say, "She's sensitive. Pull mine instead." These little things add up to make her a wonderful and caring friend.

She always reminds me to call her if I have any problems with school or my family, telling me no matter how busy she is she will squeeze in a couple of minutes to listen. She even offered to accompany me to the hospital after school when I had to go to check some personal problems.

I can always count on her to have a good time and to make me feel better when I'm down. She's a lot of fun to be with, has a great sense of humor, is witty and intelligent, and possesses just about all the qualities that make a best friend. We go to different high schools now, but we still keep in touch by phone. I may not see her every day, but I know she will always be one of the best friends I'll ever have.

GROWING UP NUYORICAN

By Jennifer Morales

For me, being Puerto Rican is a source of pride. We have a beautiful island and a unique culture that is a mix of many others. Our ancestors include the Taino Indians, the original inhabitants of the island; the Spanish, who settled on the island in the 16th century; and the Africans, who were enslaved by the Spaniards and brought to Puerto Rico to work.

You can see each of these three races in our features and skin color. In my family, we have some people who are dark and some who are fair. My aunt looks like an Indian. She has dark skin, long, black, wavy hair, and large, dark eyes. Even though they're sisters, my mother looks nothing like her. She has curly, brown hair, small, green eyes, and very light skin. Some Puerto Ricans look black, some look white, and some look brown. Not every Puerto Rican has dark hair and eyes. Some have blond or red hair with blue or green eyes.

Many people think that Puerto Rican culture is dying. Because the island is a commonwealth of the United States, our culture has become Americanized. Puerto Rican families that live in the U.S. tend to have an especially American lifestyle.

Though we keep our language, we listen to American radio stations and watch American television shows. My sister and I would rather listen to rock than salsa and merengue. We very rarely watch the Spanish TV stations.

I am not fluent in Spanish, because I speak English at home. The only time I speak Spanish is when I go to my grandparents' house, or to Puerto Rico. But at home we do eat a lot of Puerto Rican food like arroz con pollo (chicken with rice), pernil (roast pork), and ensalada de bacalao (codfish salad).

Another reason Puerto Ricans are becoming Americanized is that

23

we don't learn about our culture in school and our parents often don't teach it to us at home. I'm lucky—my mother has always told me stories about life on the island when she was little. I know a little about my culture and with the help of my mother and father, I'm trying to learn more.

I love my mother's stories about how holidays are celebrated on the island. During the winter, Puerto Ricans celebrate Christmas (La Navidad) but we also celebrate El Día de los Reyes on January 6. That's the day that the three kings (also known as the three wise men) finally reached Bethlehem and presented their gifts to baby Jesus.

On this day, Puerto Rican children collect grass and put it in a shoe box under their beds. The grass is for the kings' camels to eat. The kings then leave presents behind in place of the grass. My mother told me that when she was a little girl, everyone would decorate their homes with lights and musicians would go from house to house playing music and singing to celebrate this day.

Puerto Ricans also celebrate El Día de Todos los Santos, which is like Halloween in the United States. But on the island, instead of dressing up, everyone lights candles and there are processions through the streets. They still have these processions but now most of the people dress up in costumes like we do here.

I love to go to Puerto Rico. We have been going every year since I was a baby. It's peaceful and beautiful. I usually stay in my grandparents' home, which my grandfather built on a hill by the beach in Dorado, near San Juan. From the balcony you can see practically the whole island on a clear day. It's a beautiful sight. I feel like I belong there, but I feel a little weird sometimes when adults talk to me, because I don't speak Spanish very well. My cousin tries to help me by translating when I don't understand what someone is saying.

Even though I like visiting Puerto Rico, I don't think I could live there. I would miss New York and my friends. My mother wants to move there but I don't want to go. I like things the way they are now—a little bit of both worlds.

COLOR ME DIFFERENT

By Jamal Greene

I am black. Yet, since I was 12 I've gone to a school almost totally devoid of black people. I don't speak in slang. I don't listen to rap or reggae and, try as I might, I have at best a 50-50 chance of converting a lay-up. Except for the fact that I'm not White, I am not all that different from a stereotypical white kid from Fresh Meadows.

Because of this, when I am around other black people, I usually feel a certain distance between us. And so do they. For example, this past summer I took a journalism workshop at New York University. After it was over, I was on the phone with one of the girls in the workshop, a black girl, and we got to talking about first impressions. She said that for about the first week of the workshop, she was saying to herself, "What's wrong with this guy? Is he white or something?" She said that I talked like a "cracker" (as she put it) and she made a lot of offhand remarks about me not being a "real" black person. It irritated me that this girl thought that just because I didn't speak Black English, I was not a genuine black person.

I have often heard people criticize Yankee announcer Paul Olden for the same thing. Olden is black, but you would never know it from the way he talks. They say he's trying to be white. I don't "sound Black" either and I'm not trying to be anything but who I am. It's just the way I talk. Black people who speak standard English don't do it because they want to dissociate themselves from other black people but because they grew up hearing English spoken that way.

Just look at the English boxer Lennox Lewis. He's black but his accent is as British as can be. Is he "trying to be English" and denying his black roots? Of course not. He just grew up around people who had British accents.

I don't dance like a lot of other black people either. I never learned

to move my hips and legs the way most kids you see at parties are able to. I lose the beat if I have to move more than two body parts at once and so my dancing tends to get a little repetitive.

When I go to parties with black people I often find myself sitting at the table drinking a Coke while everybody else is dancing. "Why aren't you dancing?!" people ask. And then when I do get on the dance floor, the same people sneer at me. "What's wrong with you?" they say. "Why do you just keep doing the same thing over and over again?"

Contrary to popular belief, black people aren't born with the ability to dance and play basketball. Even though I have speed and leaping ability, I can't drive to the hole without losing my dribble. Those skills have to be learned and perfected with experience. It only seems like they are innate because the black community in America is culturally very close—knit and people share the same interests.

Another thing that constitutes "blackness" in a lot of people's minds is an interest in or a feeling of pride and identification with things historically black. I collected baseball cards until I was 15. I had a pretty substantial collection for a kid. At least, I thought I did. One afternoon, my cousins came over to my house and were looking at my baseball cards. "Do you have any Jackie Robinson cards?" one of them asked.

"Of course not," I answered.

They were visibly displeased with that response. Of course in my mind I knew that the reason I didn't have any Jackie Robinson cards was the same reason why I didn't have any Ted Williams or Mickey Mantle or Joe Dimaggio cards. I just didn't have the money for Jackie Robinson. Even if I were going to spend that money on baseball cards, I would buy a Mickey Mantle card before I would buy a Jackie Robinson card of the same price. Jackie may have been the first black major leaguer but Mickey hit home runs and home runs increase in value faster than historical novelty. It's that simple. But my cousins thought that the reason I didn't have any Jackie Robinson cards was because I didn't like black players as much as white players.

My family has always had a problem with me liking baseball—a game that did not integrate until 1947—as much as I do. They keep

getting me these Negro League postcards because they are worried that I don't know enough about the subject. And they're right. But then again, sports enthusiasts in general don't know enough about the Negro Leagues. My family feels very strongly that as a black sports fan, I should feel an added responsibility to know about black baseball players. If I don't learn about them, they say, then nobody will.

Minorities are often called upon to be the spokespeople for their races. The only black kid in the class is almost always asked to speak when the subjects of slavery or the civil rights movement come up. The question is, does he have a responsibility to know more about issues pertaining to blacks than his white classmates? I would like to think that he doesn't.

I f we really believe that everyone should be treated equally, then ideally my Jewish friends should be expected to know just as much about black history as I do. Of course I should know more about the Negro Leagues than I do now, but so should a white baseball fan or a Japanese baseball fan or a polka-dot baseball fan.

So I guess I don't fit in with the black people who speak Black English, dance with a lot of hip motion and hang out with an all-black crowd. And I don't feel any added responsibility to learn about black history or go out and associate with more

> **When I go to parties with black people I often find myself sitting at the table drinking a Coke while everybody else is dancing.**

black people either. Nor do I fit in with blacks who try as hard as they can to separate themselves from blacks altogether, vote Republican, and marry white women. I don't do that either.

Even though I grew up playing wiffleball with white kids in Park Slope instead of basketball with black kids in Bed Stuy, even though I go to a school with very few blacks, and even though most of my friends are white and Asian, I can't say that I feel completely at home with white people either. Achieving racial equality is a process that still has a long way to go. Blacks were slaves just 130 years ago. Until just 30 years ago, we were legally inferior to whites. Blacks may have achieved equality before the law but it will take another few generations to achieve social equality.

There is still a stigma attached to interracial relationships, for example, both romantic and otherwise. Whenever I'm around the parents of white friends, I get the sense that they see me not as "that nice kid who is friends with my son or daughter" but rather as "that nice black kid who is friends with my son or daughter." There is still a line that certain people are unwilling to cross.

So after all this analysis, I'm still confused about what it means to be black. What is race, anyway? According to Webster's, race is "a class or kind of people unified by a community of interests, habits, or characteristics." Well, anyone who's ever called me or any other black person "White on the inside" because we didn't fit their stereotype can look at that definition and claim victory. "There it is, right in the dictionary," they're saying. "Black is an attitude, not just a color."

> **Even though most of my friends are white and Asian, I can't say that I feel completely at home with white people either.**

By that definition I'm not black at all. But I was black the last time I looked in the mirror. So I went back to the dictionary and found that Webster's has another definition for race: "a division of mankind possessing traits that are transmissible by descent and sufficient to characterize it as a distinct human type."

Wait a minute! Does that mean that a black person is anyone with dark skin, full lips, a broad nose, and coarse hair? These are traits transmissible by descent and distinct to black people. By the second definition, to be black means to have these physical characteristics. Speaking Black English and dancing well are not genetic. They are cultural and arise from blacks living isolated from other communities.

Which definition is right? I would like to think that it is the second. I would like to think that race is nothing more than the color of your

skin, but clearly in most people's minds it's more than that. I feel distanced from blacks because I am black but don't act the part and I feel distanced from whites because I act white but don't look the part. As long as other people expect me to act a certain way because of the way I look, or to look a certain way because of the way I act, I will continue to be something of an outcast because I defy their prejudices.

Society has different expectations of blacks and whites, and becomes uncomfortable if any of us strays from those expectations. Just ask anybody who's ever picked me for two-on-two just because I was black.

FROM EXTENSIONS TO DREADLOCKS: BLACK HAIR IS BEAUTIFUL

By Zenzilé Greene

When people say "black is beautiful" I wonder whose idea of black they really mean. I sure hope it doesn't just refer to the Black women on the boxes of PCJ relaxer because for me it doesn't stop there.

Don't get me wrong. My hair used to be straight too. I got my mom to straighten it with a hot comb for about a year beginning when I was 15. I used to have extensions before that and I wanted to have my own "natural" hair for a change. The first time she did it I swore it was only a trial thing but she knew me better. I really did believe it would only be temporary, but it made my hair so manageable. Although I hate that excuse for black people straightening their hair, it is true.

The only problem was I wouldn't even peek out of my window or step outside my door unless my hair was completely up to par. I would freak when it rained. I mean I would have a fit—as if God was cursing me personally by making it rain. Water was now my enemy and I absolutely never went swimming.

Even when I was in the house my hair reacted to the weather. I couldn't stop it from springing up. My hair got thinner and started to get split ends from the constant "frying." It was horrifying. I wouldn't let anyone see me that way.

Finally, I decided I couldn't live that way anymore. It made me paranoid about my looks and it was driving me crazy. I didn't want to have to worry about my hair all the time. I decided to get dreadlocks.

I had dreads once when I was much younger but it was for a stupid reason. When my mom used to comb my hair and braid it, it was very painful and I would do anything not to endure it. I had the locks for a few years but finally got rid of them because I couldn't deal with

people's reactions anymore. Adults were overly in awe of them and kids were either utterly disgusted or jealous.

This time I knew I definitely wanted dreads. I was sick of looking like everyone else. I hate conforming. I started to feel like a complete idiot going through all this crap just so I could have my hair look like something it wasn't. I mean I wasn't born with straight hair. Why was I suddenly trying to change the course of the weather so that I wouldn't have to be burdened with what is truly me?

The summer before last I went on a vacation to Barbados and didn't want to fuss with my hair after I went swimming in the ocean. So I had my mom do my hair in tiny little braids while it was straight. I didn't mean to start my dreads off that way but whenever I got in the water my hair would get wet and "turn back," so I decided to just leave it.

My hair was pretty long when I first started my locks so now they're just bordering on shoulder length. I love them. It doesn't matter if it rains or if it's humid out, or whether I go swimming or some jerk decides to throw water at me, because my hair is completely free of all chemicals and only reacts the way it was meant to. It's hard to take care of but it's worth it.

I've had several people on the street ask what my purpose for having dreadlocks is. Basically I just wanted to prove to myself that my hair, free of

> **When people say 'black is beautiful' I wonder whose idea of black they really mean.**

chemical manipulation, is beautiful and not something to be scorned. At the same time, I want to show everyone else that, "Hey look. Kinky hair that is not permed or relaxed can be more than okay."

I'm not saying for every black girl to go and get dreadlocks. But I am saying that there are many distorted ideas of beauty imposed on us by fashion magazines and other media (you name it), ideas about fair skin, skinny bodies, long straight hair, fine features...Whether we realize it or not we all fall victim to these influences and reject ourselves in little ways.

I think it would be nice if we could each have something to com-

pensate for the parts of ourselves that we discard to fit those ideals, something all our own, culturally and/or personally. That would be the first step to accepting ourselves as a whole instead of trying to be something totally the opposite of who we really are.

AT HOME IN THE PROJECTS

By Fabiola Duvalsaint

Projects. A year ago I would have shuddered at the thought of being in one and around the people in them. I mean, people in the projects are mostly drug dealers and prostitutes anyway, right? Like most people, I didn't know any better about public housing projects because I had never been to one. But that didn't stop me from imagining what they were like.

To me, the projects were a place where dangerous people lived, a place you didn't go if you didn't live there. Basically, they were forbidden territory. I mean my neighborhood wasn't the kind with white picket fences up and down the block. For a while, my neighborhood was thought of as hard core. But unlike my neighborhood, I thought that the projects couldn't change for the better. I thought they were made for hardcore people who weren't to be messed with.

The way they made projects look on TV, how could you not be scared? The tall buildings that look all the same, the drug dealers racing each other to see who could push up on you first, and the daily shootings.

If my friends and I found out someone we knew lived in the projects, we would act like we had known it all along. If a girl passed by with "door knocker" earrings, the baggy pants with the boxers hanging out and a bandanna wrapped around her head, one of my friends would look at her and automatically say, "Here comes the projects." And everyone at our table would burst out laughing.

Then I met Maria (not her real name). We met freshman year in gym class, but we weren't really friends. Maria was tall, Hispanic, had the wild curly black hair most girls would die for, and was very blunt. If she didn't like something she would let you know it in a second. She spoke her mind and didn't care about the consequences. The following

year we had a math class together. One day, I noticed she had a cool electric blue nail polish on so I asked for the name.

She looked at me as if I was stupid and said, "It's blue." After that I was like, "Forget that! She's probably a b--ch anyway."

Then one day a girl dropped her pen in class. When she tried to get it with her foot, she got stuck. Maria and I started laughing. We were laughing so hard that the class' attention was focused on us, making us feel like we were on *Showtime at the Apollo*.

After that we just started talking like two friends who knew each other from way back. For a while during junior year we got separated. But one day we bumped into each other and decided to meet at McDonald's once a month after school. Then once a month turned into once a week and before I knew it, Maria and I were getting together every day, either to go to my house or just hang out by our school field.

One day I asked if I could come over to her house.

"You want to come over my house?" she asked, looking like I was talking in a foreign language.

"Yeah," I said. "What's the matter?"

Maria just looked at me and smiled. "I live in Vandeveer," she said.

I didn't know what that was so I asked. Again she smiled and said, "I live in the projects."

I looked to see if she was kidding, but deep inside I knew she was dead serious. Immediately, questions started popping into my head: What the hell was she so happy about? How was I going to get myself out of this situation?

I guess she could tell how I felt by looking at my face, because Maria told me right away that I didn't have to go if I didn't want to. I wanted to back out, I really did, but I sensed that not going would mean my friendship with her wasn't real somehow.

When my last class ended that day, I went to meet Maria at our usual spot (the locker room). As we started to walk, Maria looked at me and started laughing. I asked her what was so funny (because at this

point I sure needed a good laugh).

"You're scared!" she said.

I turned toward her and looked her straight in the face. "I'm not scared. Why should I be?" Great! Not only was I a coward, but I'd turned into a liar too.

I wanted to turn back, and had almost decided to, but just then Maria pointed to an orange building surrounded by other orange buildings.

"Here it is," she said.

I had been so filled with dread and my thoughts were so locked on turning back that I didn't even realize that we had already arrived. When I looked around I was shocked (I'm talking literally here). There were no hard core drug dealers on the corners and I certainly didn't hear any gunshots. This neighborhood was quiet and calm—as if all the people who lived here were hibernating inside their apartments. Was this what I was afraid of?

We crossed the street and went inside the building. When we got upstairs to her apartment, I met her mom and sister. I got so comfortable in her apartment that my fears melted away. My worries were all just gone! Her

> **The way they made projects look on TV, how could you not be scared?**

apartment was like any other and her room was just as messy as mine, which made me even more comfortable.

She had a dog named Rufus that tried to kill me when he saw me, and a quiet cat that just sat around. Her mom looked harmless. But the truth is, she would take crap from no one. She let me know on the spot that if I was going to be a bad influence on her daughter that I shouldn't think about being friends with Maria at all.

But during that afternoon, she saw that my intentions were just to be friends, not to lead Maria to the wrong side of the tracks. When it was time to leave I told her that this time I really wasn't scared and I could manage to get to the bus stop across the street on my own.

After that day I went over to Maria's house more often and my views on the projects changed (so did my taste in friends). Now I've

grown to learn the true meaning of the saying, "Believe none of what you hear and half of what you see." And I am not as ignorant as I used to be.

Note: Vanderveer is technically not a project. Public housing projects are owned by the city. Vanderveer is owned by a private company, but it looks a lot like what you might think of as a typical project. Maria and her friends consider Vanderveer "the projects."

WHERE I LIVE

GROWING UP IN EAST HARLEM

By Jeanette Melendez

I live in East Harlem in the Wagner housing project on 122nd Street and First Avenue. My neighborhood may seem dangerous to many people, but if you grew up here, it wouldn't seem that scary. It's a poor neighborhood. Most of the buildings are old and shabby housing projects or tenements.

Sometimes when I walk down the street, I feel like this is one of the most horrible places to live. The crack addicts roam around searching for drugs and sell their personal belongings to get money for crack. The crack dealers are just as bad. I used to come home from school and they would greet me at the front of my building. Their presence used to intimidate me. Nowadays they mostly work alone and a lot of them are dead.

The sounds of shattering glass and gunshots are commonplace. The police are just as much a part of this neighborhood as the people who live here, but the problem is nobody respects them. In fact, cops are the last people anyone in my neighborhood would turn to.

The main problem in my neighborhood is crack. A lot of people are addicted to it. For the users, it is the $5 high—something that lets them forget that they don't have a job or that they have to live on welfare. Life here is tough and that is how some people cope with it.

Take Alex, a boy I grew up with. He once told me that he was going to sell drugs in order to pay for college. Alex came from a good family. He lived with his parents and his brother is a doctor.

But Alex sold drugs for quite some time and never went to college. At 18, he was beaten up by about 10 Hispanics and blacks in front of the local store and, as a result, was in a coma. He was beaten so badly that no one could recognize him and I was told that sneaker marks were indented in his face. I didn't have the courage to visit him in the

hospital. Alex died this past August.

Many of the dealers have a philosophy that they think justifies selling drugs. They believe that school is a waste of time because they are black or Hispanic and won't be able to make a good living. In short, they blame it on society. Many of my friends adopt this way of thinking in order to justify leaving school, getting pregnant at 16, or selling drugs.

Drugs are not the only problem in my neighborhood. Teenage pregnancy is just as common. Most of the girls I played tag with when I was growing up are mothers. A lot of the girls latch onto their boyfriends early. Nine months later, they've got a baby because they usually don't use birth control. One of the friends I grew up with has two children and a boyfriend who is always in jail because he sells drugs. She lives off welfare and she is now waiting for her boyfriend to get out of jail again.

> **I can't claim that life here is easy. It takes a lot of courage to survive in this neighborhood.**

A lot of people think that these teenagers have been brought up wrong, but I disagree. Many parents in East Harlem are hard working and they want the best for their children. But sometimes it's beyond their control. Many teenagers see negative things in their neighborhood and assume that their situation will not be different.

There are a lot of good people in Harlem who are just as ambitious as I am. A lot of the people know where they're going and they are going to make it. However, I can't claim that life here is easy. It takes a lot of courage to survive in this neighborhood, but there are some benefits—you learn to be strong, independent, and fearless. Sometimes that's all the education some people need.

I'm glad that I was able to see another side of life. Going to Hunter College High School has made me aware of the opportunities that exist for minorities. I only wish that I could let everyone know that living in Harlem is not a death sentence.

THOMAS JEFFERSON HS: A SCHOOL DEALS WITH DEATH

By Michael Quintyne

People who haven't been to Thomas Jefferson High School think that it is hell on earth. They picture the students as drug dealers and troublemakers who all carry guns. But to Eric Alexander, 17, a senior at "Jeff," the school is more like a family.

"Most of the students treat each other with respect," said Eric. "And most of the teachers treat them as [they would] their own child."

On February 26, Eric was in the second floor hallway on his way to class when he heard the shots that left two students dead. Eric ran into the dean's office. Like most of the students, he was terrorized and confused. According to social studies teacher Sharon King, the minute the shots rang out, Principal Carol Beck came out of her office and began ushering kids into the auditorium. "She could've gotten shot," said King.

"Mrs. Beck stayed strong through the whole thing," said Melissa Baltazar, 14. "[She] is the kind of person who keeps looking forward and never looks back...I don't think the school could survive without her."

After the shooting, Melissa said there were no regular classes in session. "There were just rooms to go to and teachers would have you express your feelings so you didn't hold anything back." Even though the teachers themselves were frustrated and scared, Melissa said they didn't let it show. They had to stay strong to support the students.

Eric said many freshmen wanted to transfer out of the school right away. "The other kids were trying to persuade them not to leave because we need [their] support."

This story was published in April, 1992.

While everyone had good things to say about the school, most admitted that the streets around Thomas Jefferson are infested with drug dealers and gunmen and students are influenced by that.

"Ain't nothing wrong with the school," said Kerry Collins, 18, a senior and member of the track team. "It's just in a bad neighborhood."

King agreed. "You can get a gun on every corner in East New York," she said. "Do you see a library on every corner?"

Some kids bring trouble to school with them. "Guys come to school from different projects thinking theirs is better than others," explained Melissa. "That's what brings on the violence... The school isn't the problem it's the kids that come in."

Kerry said peer pressure often contributes to the problem. She said sometimes a guy is willing to "leave [a bad] situation alone but his friend gonna try and juice it up...call him a sissy or whatever and that will lead him into doing something [stupid]."

It will take more than guards and metal detectors to make schools really safe.

Nevertheless, students at Jefferson seem to have learned a lot from the tragedy. "Ian, [one of the boys who was shot] was popular with a lot of people," said Melissa. "When they see one of their friends die they know that it could have easily been them... Students now see that guns aren't toys...and it's changing their attitude in a more positive way."

"Many [students] are traumatized," explained King. "I think this mess is becoming more clear to them...I don't think they'd want to see this happen again. Ever. It's a hard way to learn, but they got it."

Students feel that metal detectors should have been installed long before this. After the first incident in which a Jefferson student was shot and killed in the hallway last November, the Board of Education brought in a security team with metal detectors for a surprise visit once a week. Since the second shooting last month they've been there every day. "They're doing everything they can do now," said Kerry.

Everyone I spoke to agreed metal detectors and more security

guards were important "but they should not treat us like we're in jail," Eric said. King said it upsets her to see the students searched, treated like criminals, and having to wait a half an hour to get past security in the morning.

"Security is just a band-aid to the problem," she insisted. "We need to start building character." She'd like to see more special programs, some form of "manhood training" in the curriculum, and more Black male teachers to serve as role models.

Students agree it will take more than guards and metal detectors to make schools really safe. "There were a whole lot of police patrolling the second floor where the two guys got shot," said Melissa. "It doesn't matter how many policemen or security you have around, it's just the attitude of the kids. They're the ones that are gonna change the violence that's happening in the school."

BROWNSVILLE: FINDING BALANCE ON MY BLOCK

By April Daley

It's early. The hands on the ancient clock on my kitchen wall barely scratch past the line indicating 5 a.m. It's a touch before the sun kisses the horizon, even before the young students shuffle toward the B7 bus or the #3 train down the block. I walk to the front door of my brick house to observe the short block where I've lived for 15 years.

Like I said, it's early. Maybe that's why the corner by the train station isn't yet occupied by alternating groups of police officers and young African-American men the color of coffee beans. It's too early for mischief, too early for drugs and arrests.

My eyes search the scarlet brick homes and gray sidewalk and lock on the church on the far left side of the block. Its paint is peeling and its surface has small cracks. It has reason to look old. Its life spans longer than mine and the other teenagers' here. It may even span longer than the lives of some of the adults.

Still it remains strong. Except for layers of paint, it's the same as it was when I was born here 15 years ago. It's our beat-up icon of hope on this block. Only hope can explain how it can exist on the same block as the drug-dealing corner and the families whose profanity-filled music plays at all hours of the night.

There's a balance to this block in Brownsville, Brooklyn. The innocence and goodwill of the church balance with the mischief on the opposite corner where young guys buy and sell drugs. The number of older people balances with the number of teenagers. Even the former abundance of Caribbean families has now become balanced with the recent additions of Hispanic familias.

A loud, throaty bark pierces the morning silence. I find its source

across the street—the bear-dog. I'm not sure what his real name is. My sister and I have been calling him the bear-dog since we decided that he looked like a bear with a dog's body. He barks at Mr. Joshua, the owner of the cleaners four buildings down. It's a game they play, I suppose. Mr. Joshua teases him with a subtle shake of his head and then continues down to the cleaners to open his shop for the day.

My neighborhood was primarily residential at one point, but recently new businesses have cropped up. A new barbershop opened about a year ago and then a bookstore close to that. It's like another unconscious attempt to find balance—this time between houses and businesses.

It will only be a few hours before Julie's Beauty Salon and Happy Chinese Food open on either side of Mr. Joshua's, and less time before Hope, Faith and Charity, the elementary school across from him, opens for the day. I pull on my messenger bag and head into the territory I just watched so lovingly.

As I trudge past the bus stop, I wonder about my future on this block. I wonder whether or not I'd allow my own kids to live here. I wonder about my parents and whether I would want them to live here alone after I've moved out.

I decide that, given the choice, I'd raise my family here and I'd let my parents live here alone. It isn't a wealthy neighborhood, nor is it "ghetto." It's a good enough balance between the two. It's a great block, Saratoga Avenue, between Dumont and Livonia. I wouldn't think about living anywhere else.

THE LOWER EAST SIDE: ONLY THE FACES HAVE CHANGED

By Jia Lu Yin

The Lower East Side of Manhattan has been my home for 10 years. I've always enjoyed the stores, the people, the familiarity, the smell of pickles and fish in the air. But I didn't know a lot about the area's history. So, on a hot, muggy day last summer, I headed over to the Lower East Side Tenement Museum to join a walking tour around my community. I was hoping to learn cool, neat stuff about my neighborhood that I didn't know before. Why don't you put on your walking shoes and come along?

Our fellow walkers are mostly older and Jewish. They comment on how the neighborhood has changed over the years and how a lot of stores they used to go to are no longer there.

Everywhere we walk, we notice how crowded the streets are. You have to do some quick maneuvering and fancy stepping to pass through the maze of people without stepping on or bumping into somebody. Our tour guide, Seth, tells us the neighborhood has always been this way. In 1900, the average number of people living on an acre of land in the U.S. was 65. But on the Lower East Side, there were 2,000 people per acre, making it one of the most densely populated communities in the country.

Since the neighborhood is poor, it has its problems. I'm surprised when Seth leads us over to Seward Park. I would never ever go there by myself, not even during the day. There are lots of crack vials on the ground and drunkards and drug dealers are always hanging out. Passing it now makes me sad because when I was small, I used to hang from the monkey bars and fly up to the sky on the swings with my friends.

I get even sadder when Seth informs us that Seward Park was the first urban playground for working-class immigrants. Six tenement houses had to be torn down to build it so the neighborhood's children would have some open space to play in. Maybe it's time we start pushing out the pushers and take back our park.

Next, we stop outside a grimy looking gray building, where hot steam gushes out of exhaust pipes and the bars on the windows make it impossible for us to see inside. Seth tells us that this miserable building is the site of a garment sweatshop.

Chinatown is full of these places. When Chinese immigrants first arrive in New York, they often know no English so their job options are limited. The men usually end up working in restaurants while the women make clothing in sweatshops like this one. Workers are paid by the piece, so they have to work as fast as they can. Even laboring away at breakneck speeds for 12 hours a day does not guarantee that they will be able to earn even minimum wage. In recent years a lot of Mexicans have started to work in these dangerous factories along with the Chinese.

When I was little, I used to go to these factories with my mom, thinking everything was just fun and games. I would cut threads off the garments for two cents a piece so our family could make enough money to survive. I was too small and innocent to know how unsafe and unfair these operations are.

You know those cool nylon baseball caps that everybody wears? Well many of them are made in sweatshops where workers get 18 cents a piece for doing one. Since they have to sew as fast as they can, the workers are constantly piercing their fingers with hot needles. After seven or eight years, their fingers get completely numb and they can no longer do the job.

Even very respectable, big companies use sweatshops because the labor cost is cheap. Seth told us that a single-breasted wool, silk-lined jacket costs about $58 to make, materials and labor included. A fancy store will then sell this same garment for $700! That's why using sweatshop labor is so appealing.

What I didn't know was that the Italians, the Irish, and the Jews all started out working in these factories when they first came to the Lower East Side. It just goes to show that the cycle of exploitation and poverty doesn't really end. It just quietly moves on to other victims.

After the depressing news of Chinatown sweatshops, our tour moves on to Little Italy, where sidewalk cafes take up half the street. It seems that Little Italy is getting smaller every year. These days it's mostly Chinese who move in and out of the narrow streets, not Italians. In fact, Seth told us that a lot of Italian restaurants have to pay rent to the wealthy Hong Kong businessmen who have been buying up land in the neighborhood.

Many Italian merchants started out by selling fruit, fish, and food off pushcarts on the streets. The great pastry chef Ferrara started out as a street peddler selling cannolis before making it big. Now Ferrara's restaurant serves pricey, fancy food to tourists. The street peddlers are still there, but now they're Chinese who sell everything from ginseng to vegetables. As with so many things on the Lower East Side, the script is the same. Only the ethnicity of the characters is different.

Our tour ends with a bang, or rather a roar. Lightning and thunder crash across the sky. Fat drops of rain start to fall. They wash away the garbage on the streets, but not the history of the people who have lived here.

CANDY APPLES TO CRACK VIALS: A WALK THROUGH CONEY ISLAND

By Sheila Maldonado

I live across the street from the Atlantic. Not Atlantic Avenue, not the Atlantic Deli—the Atlantic Ocean. My house is just a short block away from the Coney Island boardwalk and the beach.

Coney Island is like most of the poorer neighborhoods in New York City. It's dotted with housing projects, bodegas, Chinese food places, and empty lots littered with broken glass. Most of the people who live there are black and Latino. It's the kind of neighborhood the media like to call "high crime" or "low income." What makes it different from any other "ghetto" are the beach, the boardwalk, and, of course, the rides.

Every summer 4 million people come to Astroland, Deno's Wonder Wheel Park, and the beach. Hordes of them come rushing out of the Stillwell Avenue station and invade the neighborhood. They come in waves—wearing swimsuits, tank tops and sandals, with a cooler in one hand and a radio in the other. The cars swarm down Surf Avenue near the boardwalk, fighting each other over a handful of parking spaces.

When they leave, they leave a mess. On the wooden planks of the boardwalk, they leave chewed up ears of corn, greasy wooden shish kebob sticks, half eaten candy apples, and paper plates with leftover shrimp and french fries. The sidewalk outside Nathan's (the original hot-dog stand) is littered with napkins smeared with ketchup, mustard, and relish. And the wood of the boardwalk next to the kiddie park is stained with all the oil and grease.

The beaches are in similar condition, at least the most popular

spots—the ones right across from the rides and the aquarium and closer to Brighton. There, the beach is as flat as the boardwalk. The sand is covered with tiny, broken seashells, and packed down by the masses of people.

Farther down, near where I live, the beach is cleaner. The sand is soft and fluffy. Most people don't dare venture that deep inside Coney Island, probably because they're afraid.

If you want to get an idea of what's going on in my neighborhood, take a walk along the beach. You'll see the usual crack vials, and many a used condom left over from those hot, romantic summer nights. I've also found candles on the big rocks by the water, and feathers peeking out of the sand, still attached to dead chickens. Some of the people in the neighborhood practice Santería, a Caribbean religion that mixes African religion with Catholicism—a little like voodoo.

A few homeless people find shelter under the boardwalk; they hang up sheets and lay out their old clothes, empty cans, and plastic bags full of things they've collected on the streets. Even though the boardwalk doesn't provide them with walls, it does give them a roof over their heads. In the winter, they make fires on the beach and keep warm in tents. Some of them even have dogs, strays that probably approached them for food when they barely had any themselves.

> **I've always thought if you have to live in a bad neighborhood, live in Coney Island.**

At night, drug dealers hang out both on the boardwalk and down below. The boardwalk is kind of scary at night. It's big and quiet and lonely and you never know who or what is going to pop out at you. It's not as romantic as you might think.

But I've always thought if you have to live in a bad neighborhood, live in Coney Island. Sitting on the boardwalk or walking on the beach, you can see the entire sky. There are no buildings to block the view, no car exhaust or smoke to fog up the sky, just the sun, wrapped in a patchwork of bright colors and pastels, nodding off into the sea.

THE MAKING OF A GHETTO

By Cheryl Davis

Julissa Gonzalez knows what it's like to do without. Like a lot of people who live in the Bushwick section of Brooklyn, her parents moved to the U.S. from Puerto Rico. Since they've been in Bushwick, her parents have had trouble finding the kind of work that could support six kids.

Julissa's mom got her GED, went to community college and got her Associate's Degree. But even though she can often understand English, she can't speak it well, and hasn't found a job.

"I guess she doesn't have enough confidence to go out and get a job in education like she is interested in," Julissa said.

Her father works, but he never finished high school and he can't speak English, so it has been hard for him to find a decent job as well. His last job paid only $6 an hour. Recently he got a higher paying maintenance job, but he was only hired to work five hours a day. So the family still has to depend partly on public assistance.

When Julissa was young, she often had to go with her mother to the welfare office to translate.

"I felt kind of angry that I had to go," said Julissa, 17. "I knew the basics of English and I kind of knew how to speak back and forth from Spanish to English. But I couldn't really express fully what my parent wanted me to say."

It was also hard for Julissa to know all that her parents were going through financially.

"In elementary school, the kids were always bragging about their parents' jobs and I knew that my parents were raising me on welfare," she said. "And for the teacher to know that I had to miss school because I had to go translate at the welfare office for my parents, it was pretty humiliating to me."

Julissa's brother Jesus, 14, said it's understandable why his parents didn't really care about school when they were back in Puerto Rico. "I mean, what were they going to do, go to the college of farming?" he said. "Now they came here and you need, like, two degrees to do everything."

Jesus said that, in a way, seeing how his father has had to struggle encourages him to do his work in school. "I know that my father does not like the position that he is in at work," said Jesus.

In their neighborhood, Julissa and Jesus' family is pretty typical. Bushwick, which is right between Williamsburg and Bed-Stuy, is mostly Puerto Rican, and it's very poor. I went to Bushwick to interview some teens about their lives because I have been reporting about the census, and when I looked at the figures for Bushwick, I saw that families there are really struggling. I wanted to know how that kind of poverty affects teens.

When I went, it was a cold afternoon and everywhere I turned there were people outside on the corner, talking on their stoops or just looking around. I felt kind of insecure, like the people could actually tell that I wasn't from their neighborhood and that they were going to act on that.

When I interviewed some of the kids from the neighborhood, I found out that I'm not the only one who feels nervous walking through there. Nelson Lopez, 17, said he sees a lot of drugs and violence in his neighborhood. There are four drug spots in the basements of buildings around his way.

"People sell around the corner, where they steal and bother 'Chinos'," he said. "A lot of gangs. That's all that's here is ghetto."

"I think that there is so much violence because of stupidity," said Julissa. "When people aren't educated enough, they don't know how to handle their problems so they resort to violence."

In the last 10 years, Bushwick has changed for the better. But for kids growing up there now, the neighborhood still makes it more enticing to go outside, hang out and sell drugs than to stay in school.

When they see someone getting involved with drugs or gangs,

most people say things like: "They live in a bad neighborhood," "It was peer pressure," or, "The child's parents don't know what they are doing."

But there is a difference between problems and their roots. A lot of times, people only recognize the problems that are visible to them, like drugs, gangs, violence and basically what looks like a bad neighborhood.

The real causes of these problems run deeper. In Bushwick, little education and poor English skills have led to high unemployment and poverty. In 1990, the average income for a family there was only about $10,000—compared to $33,000 as the average in New York City, according to the census. Of the adults, only 36% were working while 38% were on public assistance.

It's not hard to see why few Bushwick residents have high-paying jobs—they don't have the education to qualify for many positions. In the part of Bushwick with the 11206 zip code, 60% of adults never graduated from high school. And only 6% of the population graduated from a four year college.

"The reason they have low incomes is because they haven't received the education or training to be qualified for high paying jobs," said Julissa. "And then they might have a family to support."

> **Few Bushwick residents have high-paying jobs because they don't have the education to qualify for many positions.**

It's hard to support kids even when both parents are working, if they have low-wage jobs, and it's even harder for families to get by if there's only one parent.

Of families in Bushwick where the kids live only with their fathers, 29% were living below the poverty level in 1990. And here comes the whammy: When kids lived only with their mothers, 62% lived in poverty. (That's why adults are always telling teen girls not to get pregnant.)

Such high poverty and unemployment lead to drugs and violence, because if people have no jobs, they're either going to sell drugs to make money, or they're going to take drugs to forget about their lives.

Having no money can be depressing and overwhelming, and sometimes people under stress just want to escape.

"People just do what they gotta do to make their money. They don't think twice," Nelson said. "Every summer something goes down. Somebody ends up getting shot."

In a neighborhood like Bushwick, many of the people who are better off make their money by selling drugs. The enticement to make fast cash can become overwhelming. That is when people resort to selling drugs—and violence comes with the territory. Many kids who live in Bushwick believe they don't have that much to look forward to. And most teenagers don't seem to be taking an alternate route to lead them out of the ghetto.

"You see youth just on the corner chilling," said Jesus. "Some of them are gangs, some of them are just friends that really don't have anything to do. And when the youth don't have nothing to do, they do what they aren't supposed to do."

A lot of them end up smoking weed and dropping out of school. Among people 18 to 24 years old in Bushwick, 45% of Blacks and 35% of Latinos smoke weed regularly, according to a study by the John Jay College of Criminal Justice.

At Bushwick HS, only 35% of students end up graduating. (The average in Brooklyn is 61%.) "Instead of going to school, they smoke weed, go to hooky parties and get pregnant," said Jesus. "They chill with their friends because the school won't care if you go or not."

Jesus said that, somewhere along the road, the students end up slacking off or dropping out. "When they come to school, they go inside to see who's in there and they basically get whoever is inside to come outside," he said. "By the end of the day, there is only a little bit of people there."

And Nelson Lopez said kids don't stay in school because there are "too much problems, too much fights, too many kids walking out of the classes and too much disrespect."

It's really hard for parents who didn't even finish high school to

feel like they can sit and preach to their child about the importance of obtaining a solid education. Nelson said his parents dropped out and he feels like they shouldn't tell him to do something that they themselves didn't do—even though he knows they mean well.

When teens drop out of Bushwick HS, they usually don't end up with a job. Of 16-to 19-year-olds who were not enrolled in school in 1990, only 15% were working—61% weren't even trying to look for work at all! Some of these teens could be in college, but many of them are not.

A lot of these teens are looking at what is around them and going after it. They very rarely see people coming home from work in their suits and ties and bragging about how much their salary is going to be this week. Instead, they see drug dealers with fast cars and girls and big chains, and they want that.

Although Bushwick is still a bad neighborhood now, it has improved a lot. In 1977, there was a blackout in Brooklyn, and riots and looting broke out. Bushwick suffered the most. Many homes were burned down and people and businesses left. Now, the vacant lots are being used to build new homes. And with welfare rolls being cut, more people are working.

Drug dealing, especially of crack, has also gone down. Crowds used to line up to buy crack on Knickerbocker Avenue. But many users have gotten tired of the drug life, and police sweeps forced much of the dealing off the street, and into basements like on Nelson's block. As crack dealing has dropped, crime rates have gone down, too. In the last six years, murders went down 72% and robberies went down 58%.

But Bushwick still needs help. It's not a "good" neighborhood, and many of the people who live there don't have the skills to get decent jobs. With so many teens dropping out of school, it doesn't look like that's going to change very soon.

Jesus said that he feels his neighborhood needs more programs for youth to keep them off the streets. "My neighborhood makes me feel like not going to school," he said. "It makes me feel like going out-

side and not doing my homework. But it also makes me want to go to school and get an education because you kind of don't want to end up like some people you know and see on the streets."

Teens like Jesus need after-school programs to encourage them and keep them more interested in school than what's outside. The neighborhood also needs a new high school, because Bushwick HS is overcrowded.

For the adults, the government should provide affordable bilingual courses in the area, and funding for job training centers. "[Adults] need to find out what they need to do to qualify for the high paying jobs that are already there," Julissa said. "They need to work together and find out what is the source of the problem, and then organize to solve that problem."

Julissa does know people who are getting the skills for better jobs by getting a college education. "I have two cousins who are teachers," said Julissa. "And I have another cousin that is a case worker in a hospital that works with children. She is still going to school right now."

Julissa hopes to follow their example. After she graduates from high school in January, Julissa hopes to attend New York University.

"I feel like there is no purpose in dropping out and putting all those years down the drain," Julissa said. "This is a very challenging goal, and I feel like I should make it."

TROUBLE IN THE 'HOOD

WHY ARE GIRLS SO MEAN?

By Anonymous

"Oh, did you see the hole in Katie's sweater? It was mad big!" This was said by one of the "friends" my classmate Katie thought she'd made several weeks earlier. As the cries of laughter poured out from the gym bleachers, Katie stood with her back to the six girls, ignoring them. It hadn't taken long for them to shove her out of the group after she'd caught an attitude with the group "leader."

Truthfully, I didn't care that they were laughing at her, because she wasn't my friend and I thought the hole was big, too. But when I found myself laughing too, I stopped and realized I was being just as mean as they were.

"Why do we girls treat each other so badly?" I wondered. We take advantage of each other, compare ourselves to each other and put each other down. We can be the most petty and fake people on the planet.

I see this a lot in school. At lunch I usually hear at least one group of girls talking about another girl they're supposedly friends with. I feel annoyed when I hear things like, "Didn't she wear those jeans two days ago?" and, "I don't know why all them boys be fiending for her 'cuz she not all that."

Luckily, my friends aren't like that. My friend Felicia always seems happy and tries to lift my spirits when I'm having a bad day. Michelle's one of the smartest and most honest people I know. And Brittany is kind and considerate. On the rare occasion that I have a problem with my friends, I feel comfortable talking to them about it because we've known each other so long. We can be completely honest with each other. We don't talk behind each other's backs, unless of course we're saying something like, "Her hair looks nice today."

Note: All names have been changed.

We weren't always honest and true to each other, though. When we were freshmen three years ago, things were different between us.

Brittany always seemed to be the one who needed the most attention. When our friend Brenda was obviously having a private conversation with her boyfriend, Brittany would go up to them and start annoying them. And she always talked on and on about her family and people we didn't know, while my friends and I sat there saying, "Uh huh," the whole time. Sometimes, I admit, I just ignored her.

One day we were all sitting together in Spanish class, where we always chatted during class. After finishing one of her long, boring stories, Brittany left to go to the bathroom. Michelle, Felicia and I looked at each other with relief.

"I was trying so hard to listen to her but she just kept talking on and on," Michelle said. "I wanted her to be quiet." We laughed.

"Yes, she's always talking about her cousin and what she did to her, when we don't even know her," I added. We kept talking about her until she returned from the bathroom. I knew it was wrong, but I felt also relieved that someone else felt the same way I did.

After that, we started to feel comfortable saying anything about her. We began talking about her out of habit. A few days later, Michelle, Felicia and I were in the lunchroom together.

Felicia said, "I don't mean to talk about Brittany's hair but do you see how it looks? She hardly has any hair coming through her ponytail." We all laughed, and Michelle used her hands to mimic how much hair came through Brittany's ponytail.

That's when I started feeling bad. Her hair was somehow more personal than whether her conversations were boring or not. It was something she couldn't control, so it felt especially mean to talk about it. I knew Brittany would never talk about me behind my back. She may be a little annoying sometimes, but she's a loyal friend. Suddenly I felt so awful I had to say something.

"You know, we shouldn't talk about Brittany like that because she's supposed to be our friend," I said. I knew they'd feel the same if they really cared about Brittany.

"Yeah, that's not right. You know, we shouldn't do that anymore," Felicia said. The mood was automatically serious and I could tell by our frowns that we meant what we said. Since then, we've never said negative things about Brittany behind her back.

I'm glad I realized how much I cared about her. Otherwise, we'd probably still be talking about Brittany to this day, or we'd have booted her from our group the way Katie got booted by her friends, and started making fun of her more. I think girls just get into a habit of talking about other girls behind their backs and end up doing it without realizing.

But why do girls act so mean? I think many girls talk about each other because they feel more powerful when they put others down. I decided to do some research to learn more about the problem.

I found out that it's not just a teenager thing. A Brigham Young University study recently found that this kind of behavior starts long before high school—girls as young as 3 and 4 exclude others and use peer pressure to get what they want. And many girls don't stop talking about each other when they become adults. Even my mom and grandmother often talk on the phone about my aunts and cousins. They may not be as mean as teenage girls, but it's still harsh sometimes.

> **I think many girls talk about each other because they feel more powerful when they put others down.**

Psychologists say girl-on-girl cruelty is actually a kind of bullying called "relational aggression." Girls are more likely than boys to bully without using their fists. When girls bully each other, they "use psychological forms that are harder to detect and easier to deny, and they can do it with a smile," said Tim Fields, co-author of *Bullycide: Death at Playtime*, a book about bullying.

I wasn't surprised to read that. This kind of meanness does seem to be unique to girls. I rarely see boys talking about each other behind their backs. I think that's because boys get their problems out in the open more quickly and don't hold grudges against each other. For example, my boyfriend Michael and his best friend Corey weren't

always friends. They met three years ago in the boys locker room. Michael thought Corey was talking about him.

"You talkin' about me?" Michael demanded. Before Corey could respond, Michael punched him. Corey stood there in shock, and everyone around them said, "He wasn't talking about you!"

Michael apologized. A few days later Corey and Michael started becoming friends and left the misunderstanding in the past. Today they're best friends. That never would've happened if they'd been girls. They'd probably just have talked about each other behind each other's back. Even if they did confront each other, I think two girls would've ended up being worst enemies, not best friends.

I still talk about other girls, but only to say positive things like, "Her outfit is nice." I figure if the only way I can be happy is by putting other girls down, then I'll never be able to face my own flaws. I'll just continue to cover them up by focusing on other girls. I don't want to fall deeper into my own insecurity and become a victim of my words. Being able to accept other girls' differences and faults makes me feel like a better, more open-minded person. And it frees me to spend more time working on myself.

WHEN THINGS GET HECTIC

By Juan Azize

Last summer I was headed to the bodega around my block to get a hero when I saw my boy Deps step to some kid I'd never seen before. Being the nosy friend that I am, I went over to see what the problem was. "Yo Deps, what's going on man?" I said.

"This n--ga got an eye problem," Deps answered.

"Whatever man," said the kid. I noticed he got scared when I came over, knowing there were two of us now and this wasn't his neighborhood.

But fighting over a bad look wasn't exactly the move. "Yo, forget about that man," I said. "He don't want no beef."

"So why he trying to scope if he don't want none?" said Deps.

"I wasn't scoping at you man," answered the kid.

"Yo man, squash this already so I could get my sandwich," I told Deps. "My stomach is growling."

"Aaiight man, just don't be trying to act like you represent around here," Deps told the kid. They both gave each other the hand along with dirty looks and slow moves.

After the fake pound, I went inside the store to get my salami and cheese and Deps tagged along. About 15 minutes later there we were chilling in front of my house. It was really hot and we were trying to throw girls in front of the hydrant and munching down that delicious hero when, all of a sudden, a blue Corolla with tinted windows rolled up in front of us.

I knew right away this was the kid Deps was riffing to. I remember the hero losing its delicious taste. The girls were still teasing us, trying to get us to chase them, when Deps tapped my leg cause he knew what time it was. Before I could yell "duck," I saw the back window roll down enough for a gun to fit through. I grabbed Deps like a reflex

and we both hit the floor at the same time two bullets hit the side of my house.

The car was long gone before me and Deps had a chance to feel burnt. All of a sudden the girls didn't want to play anymore and it wasn't that sunny. I never knew things could get to that point so fast. A dirty look setting bullets off didn't make any sense. What if they had caught us from behind? What if they had shot one of the girls? What if my mother had been standing there?

It really made me think deep. I wanted to kill those guys, I was so steamed. I was confused. I was flipping. I rode around with my friends looking for that blue Corolla for that whole week. Deps got a gun that same day hoping they were going to come back, which didn't happen.

This kind of thing goes on all the time: "Yo, you heard who got shot?" "I ran into some beef today." "Yo man, bring a shank just in case." I am sick and tired of hearing it. Violence surrounds us everywhere: school, work, even in front of your crib. That's the number one reason for deaths among teens in New York City. Kids nowadays are ready to kill each other over the dumbest things.

> **A dirty look setting bullets off didn't make any sense.**

I know a lot of kids who are scared one day they are just going to get blasted for something stupid like that. There are so many other kids out there with guns, knives, and short tempers. I live in Corona, Queens and when the weekends come I feel like I am in a battle zone. Before trooping it out to a jam I always have to make sure I am rolling with my little crew in case things get hectic. Most of the jams I've been to end up with a shootout or a rumble.

And this stuff doesn't just go down where I live. In school all the gossip in the hallway is about things happening in the streets. I know lots of people also carry weapons to school but the beef is outside most of the time. There was this time, last year in my old school, when my boy Duzer was supposed to shoot a fair one with another kid in school, so my little crew got together to keep it a fair fight.

When eighth period came we all hit the handball courts. While Duzer hopped around to get ready, I saw kids pulling shanks and hammers out of their Jansports. I knew this wasn't going to be no fair fight, fake gangstas put that out of style trying to find the easy way out.

It started to get hectic; people were getting shanked up and hammered down. I was playing it safe and taking them sucker punches every chance I had. It was an even rumble, not counting the fact that they had more weapons. (I admit I was scared to death about them hammers.)

When the 5-0's rolled up we were gone with the wind. A couple of kids couldn't run so they stayed on the floor covering their sore spots. My boy Eliester had a thin slice on his neck and had to get 11 stitches. The rest of us had shanked jackets and arms, nothing serious (thank God).

We ran to the hospital about 10 blocks away. About a half hour later, after the hype went down, I stopped Duzer in the waiting room and asked him what the beef was all about. I almost started to laugh when I heard the answer: "He was trying to tell me who I wasn't allowed to talk to," answered Duzer. "Yo, I was up on that b--ch way before that n--ga even dreamed about it."

A girl! I didn't understand. One of our boys gets sliced in the neck with 11 stitches and three other kids were left on the floor bleeding like cold. This crap was pathetic, killing each other over a girl who's probably ready to move on to the next man. Eight-tracks make better sense than that.

I am not gonna front though. If my boys get into more senseless beef, I am still going to catch their backs and I won't stop to ask them what the problem is. Adrenalin flows faster than questions, and my boys have always been there for me when I needed them without asking questions and trying to talk it out.

I guess it must be written in that invisible book that knows everything, the one where ladies go first and actions speak louder than words. The funny thing is, I follow that book. If my boys have beef again I'll be there asking mute questions that come out too late. It's

like a reflex. It shouldn't be, but it is. Your boys are your boys. I do stop to think about it, but only after it's too late, after the damage is already done.

Glossary

5-0s: *the cops, police.*

Beef: *a problem or dispute.*

Blasted: *get shot up bad.*

Bodega: *corner grocery store.*

Catch their back: *back some body up, being there for them.*

Crib: *house, apartment...the place where you live.*

Eight-track: *a form of audio storage, popular in the 1970s.*

Fair one: *a fair fight, one on one.*

Finesse: *the style or way people carry themselves.*

Front: *back down or hide from the truth, pretend to be something you're not.*

Get hectic: *get wild, violent, or out-of-hand.*

Glock: *a powerful handgun.*

Hype: *the excitement or the high feeling inside during a wild event.*

Jansport: *a brand-name of backpacks.*

Nine: *a 9mm handgun.*

Pound: *the hand change of two people when greeting.*

Represent: *the act of standing up for something, a neighborhood, a certain place, for yourself, etc.*

Riff: *to argue or dispute over something.*

Rolling deep: *hanging out with a lot of people.*

Shank: *a boxcutter or any sharp object other than a knife. Also the act of cutting someone.*

Scope: *look or stare at somebody.*

Squash: *the process of solving a problem without violence.*

Strapped: *armed with a gun.*

Trooping out to a jam: *to go to a party.*

IN TOO DEEP

By Phillip Hodge

I was in my 4th period class when a friend came in and said, "You heard about what happened outside? A kid got stabbed in the head."

I was shocked. "With a knife?" I asked.

"No, with a screwdriver," he said. I was even more shocked.

Later that day, my girlfriend told me she was there and saw what happened. "It seemed like they were play wrestling and then it got serious and one kid pulled out something and suddenly, a screwdriver was in his head," she explained. The kid didn't die, but he was in a coma for a long time.

"How can teenagers be so evil?" I thought. "What motivates actions like that?"

Then, I heard rumors that it was gang-related. For weeks last spring, students in my school were jumpy about the gang rumors. One day we were even let out an hour early, because there was a rumor that the Bloods were coming to my school to recruit. I'm not sure how many of the rumors were true, but I did start to see people joining.

Now, I know people from different gangs and they are good people, so I always wonder, why do they feel they need to be in a gang? Recently I went to Youth Force, a teen center in the Bronx, for a meeting called Legal Services for Youth, where they talked about teen violence and tried to answer the question, "Why do people join gangs?"

The adult speakers said that kids who join gangs are neglected at home, so they're looking for attention elsewhere. They said it seems like most teens join gangs because they're looking for a big family outside of their own family, and protection if needed.

The kids in the audience disagreed. They said most teens just join them to fit in, since gangs are becoming more and more popular. It's just like wanting to join the popular crowd—you're looking for a place to hang and people to hang with, something to belong to, a way to feel important. Unfortunately, gangs aren't all about hanging out as friends. Instead, they glorify violence, and gang members often get in serious trouble.

At Youth Force, I talked to Raul Rodriguez, 19, who joined the Latin Kings when he was 16 because he wanted to be like his brother. His brother, Papo, thought Raul was hanging around with the wrong crowd of friends, and that they would get him in trouble with the law.

"He said he wanted to watch my back, so he made me join," Raul said. "I always wanted to, in a way, because some of my brother's friends were mad cool, and I used to talk with them when they were over, talking about how it was being in the Kings."

Normally, if you want to be in the Latin Kings, you have to get jumped in by 10 or more people. Raul was lucky. Since his brother was already a member, they allowed him to get jumped in by three people instead. When he joined, Raul thought his life would get a lot more exciting. "I thought I would have fights with other gangs, people watching my back all the time, and I would start staying out late," he said.

When Raul got his gold and black beads, he thought he would get respect from everyone because he was in a gang. At first, though, nothing seemed to change. He still hung out with his old friends and was treated the same as before. "Papo would tell me to go home when they were about to do something," Raul said.

Then he started to get more involved. "I knew mad people, and even if I didn't know them, if they were a King, we would give each other a pound and throw up our signs," he said.

After a while, other gang members would call him up to help them jump somebody. The first time he went, he was nervous, but he said "it felt good at the same time," because he was eager to prove his gangsta status.

"A bunch of us went with our yellow flags and knocked on some kid's door. His mother answered and my boy asked for Sean. When he came out, we all jumped him," said Raul. The kid's mother called the cops, but everyone had already left by the time they came.

Being in the gang never got Raul in trouble with the cops, but it caused problems at home. When Raul's mother found out, she told him to quit or to move out. She didn't want him to get in trouble. Raul thought it was unfair that she had left Papo alone but not him, so he moved in with a friend for a few weeks. When he came back, his mother wouldn't speak to him.

Eventually, after his brother was put in jail for selling drugs, Raul quit the gang. Papo got two months and a year of parole, but he didn't quit the gang, although he doesn't hang with them as much as he once did.

Raul decided to stop because he didn't want to wind up in jail like Papo. "If I stayed I would have winded up selling, getting in trouble for something stupid," he said. Plus, his sister had a baby, and Raul said he didn't want to set a negative example for his nephew.

"I don't want my nephew to be in a gang, so if Danny would see me in a gang, he might want to be in it like I wanted to, after my brother," Raul said. Now that

> **Being in the gang never got Raul in trouble with the cops, but it caused problems at home.**

he's not a King, his mother has started talking to him again, too. But not everyone gets out before they get in trouble.

Izzy (not his real name), 16, who has been a member of the Bloods for three years, wound up in jail for 10 months for doing what he called "foolish things."

Now part of a program called City Challenge, Izzy is changing his life around. Izzy said he joined the gang because he was a quiet kid who wanted to fit in with the popular crowd in his school, and the popular kids were in gangs.

"I was going with the in-crowd. Me personally, I'm not the violent type," Izzy said. Some friends of his asked Izzy to join, and at first he

didn't think it was a good idea. He wondered, "What would my mom think? What would be the outcome of [joining] the gang?"

But when Izzy started seeing the gang expanding, he didn't want to feel left out—so he decided to join, even though his mother was his role model and he knew she would be hurt.

After a while, his mother found out from other people in the neighborhood that he was in the gang, and they got in a big fight. "She didn't really disown me, but she didn't really think it was me," Izzy said quietly.

Izzy was looking for close friendship, but that's not what he got. "I thought it was gonna be some type of unity and I found out it was something different," he said. "I would see them in the street and say, 'What's up?' But me chillin' with them, them being really friendly—it wasn't like that."

Last year, Izzy got in trouble with the law and was sent upstate to the Youth Leadership Academy (a boot-camp style prison) for 10 months. Because he was doing well in the program, Izzy was made a teen leader in a group where cadets talked through their problems. "I really was the type of person who kept quiet and you could never tell if I had problems unless I told you," Izzy said. "I guess they saw it as a sign of self-control. And they thought I could get through to people."

> **Where many teens live, they're expected to dress, talk and act like a thug.**

Many of the other teens had been locked up for several years, and in the group, they talked about how they would feel going home, and what sorts of family issues they had dealt with when they were younger. By helping others, Izzy also learned to solve his own problems. "I had issues and I shared my issues and I got feedback, and they shared and I gave feedback. It was one hand washing another," he said.

When Izzy was upstate, he started to feel confident about himself and to believe he could aspire to more than the thug life. And when adults saw how he had begun to change, they helped him out. Izzy said the staff at City Challenge have given him their home phone numbers

and been available to talk to him whenever he needed someone to listen.

"I had a lot of family support and would come to City Challenge whenever I had problems. I was always to myself and now I'm more open. It's made me strong mentally," he said. "Kids should be able to open up to older role models. It's good to find someone doing the right thing, something that's positive."

With help from a mentor at City Challenge, Izzy ended up getting a basketball scholarship to play for a private school on Long Island. He hopes that he will be able to go to college on scholarship.

Kids like Izzy and Raul join gangs because they are looking for friends and acceptance.

Izzy said going to school outside the city has changed his life. "It got me away from gangs and it's a lot different," he said. "I get more help in private school, it's more friendlier. The people congratulate you on your efforts, the things you do."

Izzy is also in the process of getting out of the Bloods. "I've got a lot of opportunities playing ball and going to school and I feel I shouldn't have to be inside a gang," he said.

A lot of kids like Izzy and Raul join gangs just because they are looking for friends and acceptance. They don't think they can find that unless they join a gang. But, like Izzy, many teens who join gangs might feel better about themselves if they were involved in more positive groups.

There are a lot of different organizations out there for youth who have positive motives, but it's harder to find out about positive groups than to join a gang. Besides, people don't want to be seen as punks, and they see it as being punkish if they join a club or program that doesn't glorify violence.

Where many teens live, they're expected to dress, talk and act like a thug. Anything else would be considered a sellout. Unfortunately,

too many people seem to think it's good living in the ghetto, not heading anywhere, staying poor, and hanging out drinking and getting into trouble. I'm not anti-hang out or anti-drink, but take it from Izzy and Raul: If that's what you live for, you're not going far.

HIS SNEAKERS, MY DREAMS

By Suzanne Joblonski

My Criminal Justice class last spring was really boring. I was always tired because it was my last class of the day. When the teacher talked about the difference between first and second degree murder, I would drift into dreamland. I would imagine what my future might be like, think of another idea for a story or poem, or of what my boyfriend and I would be doing that weekend.

Sometimes, I would stare at the sneakers of the guy who sat next to me. He had two pairs—one black, one white. Ballys, I think. I always wondered where he'd been in them, the kinds of places he went.

I'll call him Sam. He was the first person I spoke to on the first day of class. When class was over, I noticed he had forgotten his umbrella underneath his chair and I told him. He thanked me and smiled.

That was the only time I ever really spoke to Sam, even though I sat next to him five days a week. I also remember he and another girl in class were always annoying one another, and the teacher used to joke that they'd end up getting married.

At the beginning of the term, the teacher asked us to talk about ourselves and our future plans. Most of us had some kind of long-term plan. One girl wanted to be a lawyer, another a social worker, and one of the guys wanted to be a cop. Right after graduation, Sam said he was going to go into the military. After that he wanted to become a corrections officer.

Last May (I remember it as if it were five minutes ago), I was sitting in my auto shop class. The teacher looked really upset and somebody asked him what was the matter. He told us that one of his students had been shot and killed over the weekend. He mentioned the name, which sounded familiar to me. Wasn't that the guy who sat next to me in my Criminal Justice class? The only way I could be sure was

to see if he was sitting in his usual seat that afternoon. He was always there and always on time.

When I went to class, the seat was empty and everyone had tears in their eyes. My teacher broke the news to us: Sam was the student killed over the weekend. It was over something stupid—I think he stepped on someone's sneakers and they got into an argument. He was killed just two weeks after we learned about the different charges for murder.

> **I cried because he was a teenager and I was a teenager.**

I don't usually cry a lot, but this time I did. I cried because he was a teenager and I was a teenager. My tears were for the loss of one of our own. It was as bad as if he were a member of my own family. I am really scared that this won't be the last time this will happen to someone I know. It's been happening every day to my peers around the city. Teenagers are losing friends over stupid things—dirty looks, clothes, jealousy, and revenge.

I have one message for Sam's killers and for teenagers around New York City. Even if it looks hopeless, we are our world's future. Maybe if you plan ahead, you too can have something to look forward to. I know Sam did and so do I.

REVENGE IN THE 'HOOD: A DEADLY GAME

By Michelle Rodney

I was watching TV when the phone rang. It was my girlfriend Nicole. "Hey," she asked, "what you doing?"

"Nothing."

"Michelle, you won't believe what happened. Kenyatta got shot right across the street from my house."

"What?" I couldn't believe it. "I'm coming over soon," I told her and hung up the phone.

Kenyatta was a 22-year-old resident of East Flatbush, Brooklyn. He was just a regular neighborhood guy that I saw almost every day, a sweet-talking cutie that stood on the corner for a living. I guess I thought he would always be there. I guess we both did.

I left my house around 12 o'clock that afternoon to make the six block journey to Nicole's house. Halfway there I saw a guy I know named John. He was talking to another guy named Steven who, I guess, was breaking the bad news to him. Before I could get over to talk to them, John got really mad and started to yell about "how the hell could that happen." I decided to walk on.

A block later, I saw Billy, another friend of mine. He came over and kissed and hugged me and asked if I had heard the news.

"Yeah, that's really sad," I said.

"Hurry up and leave the neighborhood and go to college, alright, Michelle?"

"Put me on, what happened?"

"A car of guys rode down 51st and Clarkson around 9:30 this morning, saw Kenyatta, shot him in his chest and waited till he hit the floor and then got out the car and shot him four times in his head." After they did that, Billy told me, they just started to fire at random.

An old man got shot in his leg while getting into his car and some kid named Shaune also got shot. Billy seemed like he didn't want to go into details about why it had happened so I didn't ask. Had Kenyatta done something to those guys? I still don't know.

My eyes started to wander and I saw two men in suits walking in and out of the apartment buildings on 53rd Street, about two blocks away from the crime scene. Billy noticed what I was looking at and told me the two men were detectives. They had been there since the morning asking people questions.

"No one is going to tell them anything," is all I could say, because I knew the guys from around the way would want to take care of business themselves.

After that we really had nothing else to say to each other so we said our goodbyes. Billy hugged me tighter than the first time and told me to get to my friend's house safe.

When I got to the scene of the shooting the mood was very tense. All the guys I knew were outside smoking weed and drinking beers. It was so weird—everyone was outside and no one was making a sound. Even the cars seemed to be in whisper mode. I didn't speak to anyone because I didn't know what to say.

I rang my girlfriend's bell and went into her house and waited until she finally got dressed. Then we went outside and there was everybody standing right where I left them—sobbing, hurting, and plotting how to get revenge for their homeboy.

Everyone had tears in their eyes. Even my ex-boyfriend Flex, a guy who is as hard as a rock, crumbled. When I looked into his eyes I saw fear mixed up with so much hate—he would have sought revenge by any means necessary. That's when I came to the conclusion that I could never really love a gangster (b-boy) because they always love you and leave you and most of the time it's to the barrel of a 9-mm.

We stood on the corner for about half an hour and listened to a neighborhood friend named Latoya talk about how she still couldn't believe Kenyatta was dead because she saw him the day before, but you know—here today, gone tomorrow. Nicole and I stood on the cor-

ner in silence until a friend of ours named Bell said, "Hey, what ya'll doing standing on the corner with a bunch of hoods like us?"

I cracked a little smile for him but that definitely didn't last too long. "Nothing," I said. "What are you doing out here?"

"Waiting for you to come around." Then he gave me a little smile. But before I could give him my reply one of his friends called him over. The only thing me and Nicole actually heard Bell's friend say was that no one was going to come into our neighborhood and disrespect us without them getting theirs.

I'm so tired of people who think an eye for an eye is the answer that when Bell walked back over to us I didn't hesitate to tell him, "I'm not going to anyone's funeral, because all of y'all too young to go."

"You don't have to worry about anything," he said. "I'll outlive you. I'm going to be at least 105 years old."

That's wishful thinking. He'll be lucky if he makes it to 25, with the way all these guys out here are taking people's lives with no remorse. It's like the code of the streets—you smoke my homeboy; I'll smoke you. But does this ever solve anything? In my opinion, this never gets anyone anywhere. Don't they see that after they avenge their friend's name someone will want revenge for the injustice that their friend has been served? And then this vicious cycle continues.

> **It's like the code of the streets—you smoke my homeboy; I'll smoke you.**

In my experience, all it gets them is either severe battle wounds or a six foot hole at the local cemetery. I've seen one too many guys die by the hand of steel. It's like they never learn. What ever happened to good old-fashioned fist fighting? If you feel you have to correct something why not have a one-on-one, instead of pulling out? As the saying goes, revenge is sweet. But people who believe that should remember that it can also be deadly.

I didn't know Kenyatta that well so when I cried later that night, it really wasn't about him. It was more about me—the sheer fact that I could have been out there that morning. Or it could have been some

little kid going to school. I just sat and sobbed uncontrollably, feeling like I had no options and that there would be no end to this cycle of violence.

No one should have to feel the way I felt that night—lonely, hurt, mad, and sad. No one should feel such despair at age 17. The death of Kenyatta symbolized something for me. It showed me that the world is really a cold place to be, because after the tears dry up and the blood stain has disappeared someone else will die and there will be more blood and more tears.

No one seems to understand why I feel the way I do. People think I'm being melodramatic. But I'm not. I don't want some knucklehead to decide they don't like how I looked at them one day so they think my time here is done. The deadly game that they play takes innocent lives and I'm scared the next life they'll take will be my own.

Kenyatta isn't the only person I've known whose life was ended too soon. About a year ago something similar hit even closer to home—a friend of mine was shot and killed while two guys were trying to rob the pharmacy where he worked as a security guard. He tried to close the door on them but they pushed the gun in between the door and shot him.

> **No one should feel such despair at age 17.**

My friend was going to school and had three kids who he supported. They lost a father and a best friend. Who would have wanted to be the one to tell those kids that two uncaring men took away one of the most important people in their lives? I know I would not have wanted that job.

I don't have any solutions for the violence problem because even though I see what's going on I feel very helpless. There are people my own age who have no regard for human life. How are things supposed to get better if the teens who are doing the bad deeds don't want to admit there is a problem? No one can help them if they don't accept any help. Not their parents, their teachers, the city, or the state. If they wanted help they would throw the guns away and start doing positive things like going to school to learn, not fight.

The only things that keep me going are the fact that I'm scared of death (even though I sometimes need to be reminded why should I want to go on living), and that I'm on a quest to find a place where nothing but happy things exist. Everyone should have a place like that even if you can only go to that place for five minutes. Maybe if we start giving kids positive reinforcement from the time they're born, we might all have some hope of finding a place like that for the future.

SNITCHES GET STITCHES; ADULTS, GET REAL

By Zainab Muhammad

In my high school, there are two different worlds. In the first world are the students. In our world, respect is number one. We basically depend upon ourselves for protection. And that means defending ourselves when we have a fight—not backing down or running away. It means taking action into our own hands.

Then there is the adult world. In that world, people respect each other's space, personal belongings and opinions. Respect in their world is not confrontational, nor is it physical.

Some people might disagree with that statement because some adults act just as immature as teenagers, but usually when I am around adults, they are more respectful and well mannered. (You don't see most adults acting stupid in public, like on the bus or train.)

Unfortunately, in school, these two worlds don't mingle. An adult usually tells us not to fight and to walk away, and that's really what I'd like to be able to do. But most people who try to act "hard" in school do it because they don't want to be beat up or picked on. They don't want to become cornballs, punks or herbs.

Adults also tell us that if we're having a problem with another student, we should talk to an adult about it. Recently, when I went to talk to my principal about school violence, that's what he said. He sounded really convinced that this would help.

Maybe in his world it does, but in mine, telling an adult in the school about a confrontation can lead to your social demise. Most people live by the code that "snitches get stitches."

In some ways, it's not the adults' fault. They obviously can't make anyone tell them what happened, and most students won't. But I think that one of the reasons that there is a big gap between the students and

the staff is because they give us rules without looking at the reality we face in the hallways, the classrooms and the lunchrooms.

If we felt like they were more in touch with what's going on in our world, we might be more likely to confide in them when we have problems. Part of the reality they ignore is that we can't back down and be peaceful in an environment where that might get us beat up.

But another problem they overlook is that the staff who are hired to protect us aren't always doing their jobs the way they should. There have been times when two students will be about to fight in the classroom and the teacher will just say, "Don't fight in here. Do that in the hallway," and just close that door instead of calling the deans and having them come get the students.

The biggest problem, though, is with the security officers. In my school, there are about 11 security guards. I like most of them. They're cool and I can hang with them, tell jokes, or crack on some of the teachers. And they do break up the majority of fights. If they don't know you—like if you're a freshman—they may stop you in the hallway and ask for your program card. They'll send you to the holding room if you're cutting.

But sometimes I think they get so easy-going and friendly that students don't take them seriously anymore. When they become friends with you, you know you'll get better treatment, so it's easier to slack. If you get in a fight, they'll put their arm around you, and rub your back and help you calm down—which is cool. And sometimes if the security guards see people doing something wrong, they might pull them to the side and give them some advice, which can actually help.

But they might also leave out important incriminating details about a fight in their report to the dean, and they're less likely to stop you for minor violations. They want to make friends with the students so they don't seem so authoritarian. But I only see them as fake cops with flashlights who don't have much authority.

And that's not good when someone's really in danger. That's when the security guards need to stop being so friendly and start doing their jobs, taking people down to the dean or, if it's really serious, taking

them to the cops.

Now I'm not saying I want the military in our school. Actually, recently they put some cops inside and outside my school, and I discovered that I really don't like having them here. At first, I thought they might help. But after about two weeks, I started not to like their presence.

They would threaten to take us to jail for the stupidest things, like stealing someone's hat. And they were at almost all the stores near our school, which eliminated the hangout spots. That is when I realized I liked the security guards better.

Still, I think there needs to be a happy medium. I think the security guards need to be better trained, and stop slacking a bit, and the cops need to stop acting so much like dictators.

The security guards need to be better trained, and stop slacking.

My whole school needs to find a happy medium, too. School policy needs to get stricter. I believe that if you have one fight and it does not involve any weapons, you should be sent to mediation and that's it. But if you have two fights, and you were responsible for starting them, then you should be suspended. And you should be suspended for a long time, or expelled, if you fight more than three times, or your fight involves a weapon.

I don't understand why some people in my school who always have fights are still allowed to come back. Maybe that sounds harsh, but if some of the worst troublemakers weren't allowed to remain in our school, or if their behavior was kept in check, then maybe the rest of us wouldn't have to run around acting so tough, and those of us who wanted it could get an education.

At the same time, I think our teachers and administrators need to become more like our friends, so we might really turn to them when we had a problem. We need teachers and administrators who we can relate to and who understand what we are going through, so we can trust them enough to really talk to them if we have a problem.

A perfect example of that would be my old global teacher.

Although he was nice and playful, he also let us know that he would fail us if we did not do what we were supposed to do. In that class, there was never a fight and everyone respected each other (which is very unusual in my school).

I think that happened because he would talk to us with respect and he would always relate the lessons in class to our everyday lives. There were times when people in class wanted to kill each other. But he found ways for us to overcome that.

He would make jokes about the lesson or just give up-front good advice, and somehow we would eventually forget about what happened. He's the kind of adult I might feel comfortable turning to if I had a problem—the kind of adult I'd know I could trust.

I think schools need to establish programs where both students and teachers can develop closer bonds. Ultimately, it would make coming to school more pleasant for both the teachers and the students, and it might bring our two worlds closer.

I know that if we, the students, want to be treated as adults, then we have to start acting like adults. But I also think that the staff needs to get a taste of our reality before they make up the rules that they ask us to live by.

TURNING IN A KILLER

By Anonymous

About two years ago, I attended a summer camp in Crown Heights. As the summer went by I became close to a guy named George. He had many enemies. Guys were jealous of him because he had money, gear and girls. One particular kid, Sean, didn't like George. Sean and his friends constantly accused George of messing around with their girlfriends. One day, after camp, Sean and his friends attacked George and robbed him and shot him. They left him for dead just two blocks from the camp. Everyone knew it was Sean, but nobody wanted to put their life on the line.

I didn't want to say anything either, but as the days passed it picked and ate at my brain and my conscience grew louder with every thought of George. I cried myself to sleep every night. Then I saw Sean sporting one of George's chains. I snapped when I saw that. Still no one else came forward to tell. After being questioned for the umpteenth time, I broke down in tears as I told the detective and cop what I knew, heard, and saw.

My parents and George's were the only ones who knew it was me. It took almost two weeks and a lot of guts to do it because I feared for my life. But to this day I'm proud and glad I did. I'm positively sure George would have done the same for me.

George, I love and miss you.

R.I.P.

Note: The names in this essay have been changed.

CAUGHT IN THE ACT

By Rance Scully

One night a couple of summers ago, three of my friends and I were walking home from a party in Flatbush, Brooklyn. It was around midnight and there was nobody around and no cars passing by. Then we realized that a patrol car was following about 50 feet behind us.

We knew we weren't talking loud enough to be disturbing anyone or doing anything else wrong, so we tried not to pay too much attention. But when I glanced over my shoulder the car was still there and getting even closer.

"Come on guys, let's get out of here," said one of my friends.

"Are you crazy?" I replied. "If we run, they'll definitely think we did something wrong."

It was obvious that they were watching us so I came out with another idea: "Why don't we go up to them and try and make conversation?" I said.

"What?" said one of my friends. "You must be out of your mind."

"What's wrong with that?" I said. "I'll do all the talking. I'll tell them where we're coming from and that we're on our way home." I was newly arrived from Jamaica and still had a lot to learn about life in New York.

My friends reluctantly agreed, and I turned around and headed in the direction of the patrol car. Suddenly, a blinding light shined on us and a voice on a loudspeaker ordered us to put our hands in the air and spread our legs. Three cops got out of the car with guns drawn and pointed at us. I was scared and did what I was told.

"What do you guys think you're doing?" said one of them in a loud and aggressive tone.

I started to say something, but he told me to shut up and speak

when I was spoken to. They placed their guns back into their holsters and searched us thoroughly. Then they ordered us to put our hands back down.

"Tell me where some of the players are around here and we won't arrest you," said another one.

"Excuse me, officer," I said. "I don't know what you're talking about."

The three of them talked amongst themselves for a long time and then got into their car and sped off without another word. That was my first encounter with the New York City Police Department, and trust me, I was so pissed off that I promised myself I would have nothing to do with them ever again.

A DAY AT THE 63RD PRECINCT STATION CHANGED MY VIEW OF THE POLICE

By Nicole Burrowes

When I first walked into the 63rd Precinct police station, it didn't look like a station at all—at least not like the ones I had seen on television.

There was no rustling of papers, no interrogations going on, no slamming a handcuffed suspect into some overcrowded jail cell, no sergeant yelling at an officer for not going by the "book"—nothing like that at all. It was much more quiet.

What was I doing there? No, I wasn't arrested for killing my sister (although one day I probably will be). I had won an essay contest sponsored by the Police Athletic League. I had to write about what I would do, if I were Police Commissioner, to ease the tensions among the diverse communities in New York City. There was a winner for each precinct, who would be Precinct Captain for the day. The grand prize winner got to be Police Commissioner for a day. There was an awards ceremony, after which winners were taken to their designated place of office.

At the 63rd Precinct I learned a lot about police procedures. For example, the forms officers have to fill out and the codes they have to know. There is a code number for just about every crime. This way they don't have to explain the crime on the radio, they just call it by code. We rode around in the police car and listened to the C.B. radio.

They also have different code names for the different sections of each neighborhood. I live in what they call Sector George.

For undercover cops, there's a different code color every day for security reasons. This color is announced at roll call. At roll call all the officers were lined up at attention. One of them said that the captain

had some announcements. I walked in wearing my police hat and captain's jacket, and with my head held high, I made the announcements. One police woman couldn't hold it in—she just started cracking up. Then everyone started laughing.

I must admit, I did look quite funny—a high school student in an oversized police hat, and jacket sleeves hanging way below my knuckles, pounding on the podium, speaking "police talk" and not having any idea what I was saying.

Later on that day they spoke to me about becoming a police officer, and answered most of the questions that I had. They told me about the benefits of being a cop, like good pay and vacations. But they also told me about the other side. They have to risk their lives on a daily basis, a lot of people don't respect them, and they are often hated by the general public.

I had practically lost respect for them, but this visit gave me a renewed respect for most police officers. This visit also gave me a more humanized view of the police. I realized that under that blue uniform is a person—not some unfeeling robot.

EATING AROUND THE BLOCK

MY 'HOOD IS BAD FOR MY HEALTH

By Pauline Gordon

Every afternoon my abuela (grandmother) walks down the squeaky steps leading to our kitchen. When she hops into that apron, I know it's my cue to run for cover.

Making up her own recipes is how my abuela relieves her stress. She puts all her worries behind her when she takes on her mission: What's for dinner?

With a dash of this and a sprinkle of that her creations are ready. I admit that my abuela performs miracles. She stretches her budget by mixing leftovers with fresh foods, is obsessed with cooking pork in every meal, adds plenty of grease and oil—and people savor every last taste. I think it's disgusting.

My abuela is always talking about how to save a dollar. She's collected a huge stack of rusty, beat-up cans of food from the church pantry. She also frequents the tons of 99¢ stores that have opened in my neighborhood. My grandmother brings home 99¢ juice, sodas and junk foods that taste like complete crap and have no nutritional value.

I get angry and frustrated with this woman. Why is she so hard headed? She talks about saving a dollar, but if we have enough money for Direct TV and all the HBO channels she orders, I think we can afford some healthier, fresher food, instead of eating like it's hard times.

But if I complain to my abuela, she looks at me with disappointment and says, "Well, you don't know what it is to not have. It's called survival."

Like many people in my neighborhood, my abuela comes from a really poor background. Putting food on the table was an everyday struggle in her family. Every bit of food was considered a blessing.

Moving to the U.S. from Panama has been a big transition for her. Every day she sees food going to waste, while people in poor countries are starving. I understand my grandmother's attitude, but at times she acts as if we're standing directly on the poverty line, when I know that we could spend our money on food if we saved it somewhere else.

I think what we put in our bodies should be one of my family's biggest concerns. I began feeling conscious of how I eat last spring, when I started noticing how depressed and moody I was.

A friend told me that "You are what you eat" is not just a saying, but that what you eat really can affect your performance in everyday life. If you're eating a lot of sugary foods, your mood can swing wildly, or if you're eating too much you can feel drowsy and bored.

> **The more I drank it, the better it began to taste.**

At that time, my face was breaking out and my stomach was never agreeing with me. I would wake up nauseous, and get severe headaches that left me looking like an insane witch by the end of the day. I know what's healthy and what isn't, but I was constantly eating junk at fast food restaurants or running to the corner store for a pint of Haagen Dazs every time I felt depressed.

Over the summer, I joined a nutrition workshop. When I began reading the nutritional facts on the back of cartons, I started thinking about the vitamins, fat and protein that each food has to offer. I stopped going to the corner store for candy every time I had spare change.

Then we got to buy a week's worth of healthy food. I took my healthy week seriously. I drank tons more water and ate more veggies. I started using substitutes for sugar, like honey and fruits. Whenever I had an urgent craving for a sweet, crispy, layered cheese danish, I settled for a granola bar or a tall glass of vanilla soy milk.

My first time drinking soy milk was not easy. When I tasted it, I immediately spat it out. But because I felt it was a step toward improving my health, I began to drink a glass each day. My taste buds adapted. The more I drank it, the better it began to taste.

Now I'm a soy fan. Every time my abuela goes to the supermarket,

I beg her to buy me soy milk. Sometimes she'll refuse and say it's too expensive. So I put aside money to buy my soy milk every week.

Though healthy eating took an adjustment, I was feeling great! No more of that oily feeling I would get when I ate greasy foods. After an icy glass of soy milk, I felt like I could take on the world.

I also began taking nature walks around a big park, enjoying Earth's green kingdom. It felt good to take care of myself. I loved thinking about healthy foods nourishing every inch of me. I felt like I was doing myself a favor, so I vowed to continue to eat healthier.

But eating healthy in my neighborhood—Brownsville—is a challenge. My neighborhood is grim, with worn down and torn looking houses and projects surrounded by nothing but fast food restaurants, Chinese take-outs and fried chicken spots filled with miserable obese people.

Sure the food is cheap. There's a bargain everywhere you go. But you're only getting what you pay for—unhealthy processed and fried food. The Kennedy Fried Chicken place even gives out free sodas with every meal. Why can't they give out bottled water or juice for a change?

I know why people eat in those places. If you're looking for a meal that fills you up for cheap, you can go to Wendy's and buy up the dollar menu—the more the merrier—or eat at the Chinese restaurants. You can buy only junk if you're hungry without much in your wallet.

As much as I want to stay healthy, I hate having to stretch $5 to buy a meal. Sometimes I buy an Ensure and a banana nut muffin, or a veggie slice from the pizza store, and find myself hungry in an hour.

I'm proud of myself for trying to eat healthy despite my budget. But my abuela has been quite upset with my new diet. She feels my new way of eating healthy is a cry of hunger, because I've lost a little weight. She looks at me and says, "Pauline, why is your face so pale? You look so skinny! The only piece of fat you got there is that little bump called a behind."

Not so thrilled with the comment, I leave the room as she laughs up a storm. My grandma defines healthy people as those with meat, and glowing skin and hair. In her eyes, I'm bony and making a fool out of myself by not eating the food she serves. Food is food. There is no such thing as bad or good. You eat when you have and starve when you don't.

For now, my abuela laughs and figures I'll learn. But I long for the fresh taste of organic fruit on my tongue. Opening my refrigerator brings me back to the cold taste of reality: Bread full of mold, a pack of nearly rotten sausages, microwave dinners, and of bunch of God knows what decaying in a plastic container for who knows how long.

Eyes see, brain picks up data, stomach growls in response. With that I go to bed, another night of an unsatisfied stomach. I lie in bed wishing it would all go away: Poverty, my neighborhood, my grandmother's cooking, my headache.

Why are healthy foods out of reach of the poor?

Maybe I'm ungrateful or stubborn. (Why can't I just give in and eat unhealthy food like everyone else does? Hey, at least there's more on your plate.) But my anger bursts like a cannon scattering balls of depression. Why is my neighborhood such a threat to our health? Why are healthy foods out of reach of the poor? We all know people who are suffering because of their eating habits—they're dealing with diabetes, high cholesterol, or hypertension.

As darkness falls, my stomach's growling leads my mind through twists and turns. "You're hungry," I tell myself. "Get something to eat. That's better than no food at all."

Finally I scurry down to our kitchen, ignoring the tall tower of dishes in the sink and the mountains of crumbs and the stains splattered about the kitchen counter. Opening the refrigerator door, a silhouette gleaming in the light catches my eye. It's a box of soy milk. Abuela must have bought it for me!

I pick it up with relief and remember the discussion I had with my abuela days ago about my newfound love of soy. Usually our discussions end with the "I'm the adult and you're the child" theme, but to my surprise, she listened for a change.

CHEW ON THIS:
HOW I QUIT FAST FOOD. . .
AND LIVED TO WRITE ABOUT IT

By Carmen Rios

Until I read *Chew On This: Everything You Don't Want to Know About Fast Food*, a new book for young people by Eric Schlosser and Charles Wilson about what we eat, I was one of the many teens eating fast food almost every day. I loved fast food. Eating it was like getting a special gift.

By the time I was in middle school, I'd gotten so tired of eating the Latin food my mom made every day: arroz blanco con abichuelas (white rice with beans) and pollo frito (fried chicken). I preferred McDonald's. I knew that eating too much fast food could make me fat, but I didn't see myself getting any bigger (I only weigh 105 pounds). Plus, the food was delicious.

I wanted to eat McDonald's every day but I couldn't afford it. So I waited until every Wednesday, when my stepfather got paid, and every Friday, when my mother got paid. I'd go to school excited on those days because at the sound of the bell, I'd be going home to get at least $6 to spend at McDonald's.

My sister and I would rush out of the house and speed walk down our block, turn right and walk three blocks to our neighborhood McDonald's. On our way there, we'd anxiously talk about what we wanted to eat. The Big Mac meal was our favorite and we almost never got tired of it.

But when I craved chicken, I'd order the five piece Chicken Selects meal and my sister would order a "Number 2," the meal with two cheeseburgers, fries and a beverage (we always chose Coke). All we had to do next was choose the size of the meal (usually medium). After we ate, sometimes we'd get back in line and order apple pies and

a medium vanilla shake.

After I got a job last January, I promised myself that I wouldn't waste my money on fast food because I didn't want to get fat. I also wanted to spend my money on clothes and things to decorate my room. But the food was so hard to resist. Right after I got my paycheck every other Friday, I'd stop at a McDonald's or KFC. The next day, I'd bring my sister and my friend along with me and buy them lunch.

Sometimes I'd spend half my paycheck on fast food. I'd spend $6 one day and another $6 the next. Then I'd get hungry in the middle of the night and my sister and I would head out to McDonald's for a late night meal (it's open until 1 a.m.).

Once I spent my whole paycheck ($135) on fast food. It started off with me buying just one meal. The next day, I asked myself, "What's another $6?" And in the end, I thought to myself, "I wasted everything else on food. What's the point of saving $20?" Might as well waste that on food, too!

Sometimes I'd eat at McDonald's every single day, and not even the movie *Super Size Me*, about a man who only ate McDonald's food every day, scared me into stopping. The movie started off with a perfectly healthy person and ended with the same person—except that he was fat and had heart problems, all because he ate every meal at McDonald's.

In fact, the movie made me crave McDonald's. I watched the guy ordering a meal and I could almost smell the French fries and taste the Big Mac sauce. I wanted so badly to eat his food.

When I saw him throwing up, I told myself the movie was unreal. Who actually eats McDonald's three times a day every day and "super sizes" the meal whenever they're asked if they want the largest meal size? I usually ate fast food two or three times per week, and I never super sized anything. "It's no wonder he got sick!" I told myself.

But then I read *Chew On This* last April. The book disgusted me to the point of wanting to throw up. I was shocked to learn about how the animals we eat in these fast food restaurants are killed.

First, the chickens are fed a grayish mixture of old pretzels and

cookies covered with a layer of fat to make them gain more weight, according to the book. This causes many chickens to die of a heart attack. The rest are tied upside down by their legs to a chain and thrown into a tank of water that's charged with electricity.

That's supposed to make them unconscious, but the chickens that aren't properly shocked have to live through the rest. They're carried to a blade that slits their throats. Then they're dunked into a tank of boiling water.

Cows that are turned into hamburger meat are also badly mistreated. They're placed in feedlots. One feedlot can hold up to 100,000 cattle, which means the cows are crowded very close together. They don't eat fresh, green grass. Instead, they are fed special grain designed to fatten them quickly. I cried when I read about this cruelty. I couldn't believe I was a part of it.

The book also made me worry about obesity, which I've learned is a condition characterized by excessive body fat. It's a growing problem in this country. Did you know that there are 110,000 deaths every year related to obesity? (People who are obese can develop diabetes and other health problems.)

I was shocked to learn about how the animals we eat in these fast food restaurants are killed.

I believe the obesity problem is connected to the number of McDonald's around the world—31,000 restaurants in 120 countries—and their cheap prices.

A McDonald's Big Mac meal didn't sound tempting or delicious anymore. Every time I thought of eating in a fast food restaurant, I couldn't help but think of the cows and chickens. It made me feel guilty and nauseous. Right after finishing the book in April, I changed the way I eat. I haven't been back to McDonald's, not even once.

Instead I've been going to Subway and ordering the 6-inch meatball sandwich on Italian bread, with American cheese, lettuce and tomato. I thought that Subway would be a fresh and healthy alternative to Big Macs and fries. But in an interview with *Chew On This* co-author Chuck Wilson, I learned that my Subway meatballs probably came from the same factories as McDonald's hamburger meat.

Now, I'm confused about what I can eat. There are no restaurants in my neighborhood, Sunset Park, where I can eat healthy food. Even if there were, I've learned from experience that eating healthy usually means eating something that I think tastes disgusting.

Still, when I get hungry during the night, I make myself a salad or I eat fruit that my mom or I bought. I still get to eat what I want, but I make sure I'm not overdoing it. I feel much better about myself and I feel healthier—fresh, clean and not as heavy. And with the extra money I have, I can buy more clothes, shoes and beauty supplies.

I haven't given up all junk food—yet. I think it'll be difficult for me to give up soda and candy because I like to drink Pepsi and eat Snickers bars. But I bet I'll end up cutting down on junk food slowly, thanks to this book. And I'll make sure that any child I have doesn't fall into the hands of McDonald's.

> **I haven't given up all junk food—yet.**

I don't think McDonald's should take all the blame for the increase in obesity and health problems across the country, though. Adults can choose if they want to eat McDonald's or not. Nobody is forcing them. They can say no at any moment, just like I did. Most people know what eating fast food can do to them, but they still continue to eat it.

But I don't think McDonald's should advertise to kids anymore. If kids eat McDonald's when they are toddlers, they are likely to eat it for the rest of their lives, according to the book. If this happens, animals will keep getting treated badly and the earth will be populated with obese people.

Chew On This definitely made me think about what I eat. "The title of the book, Chew On This, says it all," said co-author Charles Wilson. "We just want kids to think about something they take for granted in everyday life."

So that's what I'm trying to do. Eric Schlosser, the book's other author, told me I don't have to stop eating fast food but I should treat it like a special treat. "You don't want to die," he told me in a recent

interview. "You want to do everything you can to live a good, long, healthy life. That means knowing what you eat."

PUT YOUR MONEY WHERE YOUR MOUTH IS: TEENS LEARN TO FIGHT FOR GOOD FOOD

By Natelegé Whaley

Did you know that almost one-third of New York City public high school students are either overweight or obese? There are many reasons—lack of exercise, overeating, but a big one is that in poor neighborhoods, healthy, nutritious food isn't always readily available.

When I go to "white" neighborhoods like Park Slope, I see stores with healthy food choices and cafes where people can mingle and eat outside on nice summer days.

But in lower-income neighborhoods like Bedford Stuyvesant and Crown Heights, when I walk into a local corner store, I see shelves stacked with chips, candy bars and cookies. It seems like people in my neighborhood accept the idea that junk food is the normal thing to eat, and that healthy food is "white food." But b-healthy!, a New York City-based health awareness organization, wants to change this perception, starting with teens.

b-healthy! is a training program that works with teens at The Door, a youth development agency in Manhattan. Teens attend workshops on health and nutrition, learn about alternatives to junk food and fast food, and master basic cooking techniques.

Ronny Sedura, 16, of Norman Thomas HS, said he decided to attend b-healthy's CHOP (Creating Healthy Organic Power) Project two years ago because he plays baseball and wants to stay healthy. He says he's learned a lot about health and nutrition and he's started to pay more attention to how fast food affects him. "If you eat at McDonald's you feel more down," he explained. "If you eat a home-cooked meal, you feel more alive, and have more energy."

He hasn't completely cut out McDonald's—he admits he still eats

the fries. But he's made some changes in his diet, including drinking vitamin water instead of soda, snacking on peanuts instead of Skittles, and eating more home-cooked meals instead of fast food. After two years at b-healthy!, Ronny says he's noticed the change in his body and his baseball game. "I was fatter," he said. "I couldn't run around the field and now I can run a lot."

But Ronny said that while he's making better food choices, other people in his community haven't gotten there yet. "In Washington Heights where I live there are two health food stores," he said. "They don't go because the prices are high."

Some people might argue that organic, healthy food is too expensive and that they can't afford it. I used to think the same thing. But after I talked to Elizabeth Johnson and Ludie Minaya, the coordinators of b-healthy's CHOP projects, my opinion changed. They say the amount you're willing to spend on food is often a matter of priorities.

"People's values are messed up," Ludie said. "People spend more money on their cars than their bodies."

I had to agree. There's nothing wrong with wanting some McDonald's once in awhile. But I always see people driving Cadillacs into a Wendy's. That makes no sense. If they're willing to spend their money on a fancy car, there's no excuse not to buy better food for themselves and their families.

Healthy food isn't as expensive or hard to find as you might think.

"In the way that you spend your money you're making a political choice," Elizabeth said. She explained that by spending your money on healthier foods and not fast food, you're showing that you want the best fresh food. And healthy food isn't as expensive or hard to find as you might think. You can shop more carefully in the fruit and vegetable section of your local supermarket. Or during the summer, you can go to your nearest farmer's market. Or join a Community Supported Agriculture (CSA) program [See next story, "Better Than Big Macs."]

Elizabeth pointed out that fast food restaurants try to convince people that good food is expensive and fast food is cheap. But she says you shouldn't believe it. Buying fresh foods at a grocery store, CSA or farmer's market is actually a better bargain. You might spend about $25 for a family of 4 at McDonald's, Elizabeth explained. But if you go to the grocery store and spend about $75, the food will last longer, since you can prepare multiple meals from it.

Food choices can affect an entire community's health. African-Americans, Latinos and Native Americans are two to three times more likely to get type 2 diabetes than whites, and it's on the rise in children and adolescents, according to the Centers for Disease Control.

The condition is linked to obesity, so if people began making healthier food choices they might lower their chances of getting it. "Don't think it's normal to grow up waiting to get [type 2] diabetes," said Ludie.

Now that I understand how eating fast food can affect how healthy I'll be when I'm older, I've cut back on it. By eating healthy meals my mom prepares at home, I've saved money and I have more energy. And no matter how much healthy food may cost, I can't put a price limit on food that's good for my body. Like Ludie said, "Once you start to think, 'This [fast] food is poisoning my mind, spirit, body,' you realize in the long-run it's worth it to take the time to make good food."

BETTER THAN BIG MACS

By Natelegé Whaley

Another way to get affordable, healthy food wherever you live is to join a community supported agriculture program (CSA), which gives city dwellers easy access to fresh vegetables grown by local farmers.

Here's how they work:

First, a community pairs up with a local farm. Community members buy shares in the farm, and the money goes toward paying the farmers for their crops. In return, community members get fresh food from the farm every week from June to November. Members pick up their box of food each week at a designated site—usually a church or community center.

There are more than 30 CSAs throughout the city, including in the South Bronx, East New York and Harlem. And there are payment options for all income levels—installments, one lump sum or food stamps. Some CSAs offer loans or reduced-price plans.

The CSA near my school in Clinton Hill, Brooklyn, offers two plans depending on your income. Families of two or more people with annual incomes of more than $30,000 pay $390 each year for their share in the farm. But families who make less than $30,000 a year pay $240 for their yearly share. That may still sound like a lot, but it ends up being about $10 a week—about the price of three Big Macs—for a week's worth of vegetables.

Families collect their food at a local elementary school. Each delivery contains seven to ten types of vegetables, enough to feed two to three people for a week. Over the season, members get at least 40 different types of fresh vegetables that are usually organic, and the selection changes seasonly.

To learn how to join a CSA near you, or for a list of the different locations, go to www.justfood.org/csa/locations.

FRESH FROM THE FARM

By Natelegé Whaley

Walking into the farmer's market at Grand Army Plaza in Brooklyn, the first thing I noticed was the sweet smell of apples. There were tents lined with tables of fruits, vegetables, bread and muffins for sale. The market was bustling with customers who seemed to be doing their weekly shopping.

Farmer's markets are outdoor markets where local farmers sell their products. They're held in parks, parking lots and other open spaces. Most of the city's 54 farmer's markets operate once or twice a week.

I checked out the prices at the Grand Army Plaza market. Not only did the produce look fresher than what I usually see at the grocery store, it was cheaper. Those sweet-smelling apples cost $1.25 per pound compared to $2.49 per pound at my local grocery store.

Families enrolled in the Women's, Infants and Children Program (WIC) or the Senior Nutrition Program can use special Farmer's Market Nutrition Program (FMNP) checks (which they get in addition to their regular WIC benefits) to pay for fruits and vegetables at farmer's markets.

Many farmer's markets in the city also accept EBT (electronic benefit transfer cards), otherwise known as food stamps. You swipe your card at a main terminal at the market to get tokens to use at any stand at the market.

More than $800,000 in FMNP coupons were redeemed at Greenmarket in 2000, according to the Council on the Environment of New York City, the organization that runs the city's farmer's markets.

For more information or to find your local farmer's market, visit www.cenyc.org.

MAKING IT, MAKING A DIFFERENCE

DROP-OUT BLUES

By Diana Moreno

My life as a drop out...where do I begin?

I guess you could say that I came to a fork in a road and chose to follow the wrong path to reach my goal—you know, a short cut. I thought I had found an easy way out from the hard work I dreaded. But I learned there is no such thing as a short cut, an easy way out—you have to work hard in order to make it. I guess that's why I'm here now telling you what dropping out of school was like for me, and why I decided to return.

I'm in school now because I've decided that I want to have that diploma to wave around like a gold medal. I have set myself up with a goal to graduate high school—and that's what I'm going to do. It isn't always easy, and I still think about dropping out. Sometimes I feel like I always have that white surrender flag flapping in the air and I feel like a loser and that I'm not going to make it.

But then I think of my family, the ones who always say, "I told you so," and I snap and realize I can't do that to myself. Then I try to crawl out of that big black gaping hole that I have dug for myself.

So let me get back to the story and tell you a little about myself and my school mess-up. First off, before you read this and think, "Hell, she's one of those girls who probably never made it past junior high school without the help of the soft teachers," I just have to prove you wrong.

Growing up, I was basically your average bookworm, or what my peers used to call me—a NERD. I always had my hand up in class. If I passed a test, I didn't mind showing it off. Kids called me a geek because I didn't just turn in my homework, I did extra credit, too.

I liked school, and the first time I dropped out, at the start of my freshman year, it was more of an accident. I had just moved to the

Bronx to live with my mom, but I was supposed to be attending a school in Brooklyn, and the travel time was hectic. So I tried to transfer out.

My mom had all the papers, but I was told that it was too late to transfer and I would have to wait for the February term to begin. At the time, my mom, well, she was in another world. She had her own problems to deal with. And with no one making sure I got my act together, I just let everything slide.

In fact, I wound up staying out of school for the whole year. I kind of enjoyed myself in the beginning. But the fun came to a halt when the warm days began to fade.

I found myself constantly alone—everyone was moving on and I was just sitting still while the action passed me by. I would be home doing nothing, gaining weight, lying in bed watching TV or reading, while my friends were in school, and I would hope for 3 o'clock to hurry up and come so that I could go and chill.

> **I was just sitting still while the action passed me by.**

What's amazing is that after a few weeks I found myself craving school and wanting to make my brain bigger. I would actually go and do my friend's brother's homework. I used to get all hyped when he told me he got an A or B plus on an assignment I did for him. At first, I didn't mind too much that he was getting credit for my work because I had a crush on him. But later I decided that he'd better do his own work, and I went back to being bored.

There wasn't much I could do during the day. I was scared to go outside because I was underage and didn't want the cops to pick me up and put my mom in problems. I didn't want to go outside because it was already starting to get cold and always looking like it was going to rain.

I didn't like going outside if no one was around—it bothered me knowing that my friends were in school while I was home slowly deteriorating.

I found myself reading books with words I'd never heard of and

looking up the meanings so I'd understand and develop my vocabulary. I liked to find ways to use my new-found knowledge in my sentences and have people comment, "Hey, you're a smart kid." But I dreaded what came next: "Then why aren't you in school?" Someone always found a way to bust my bubble.

I began to feel that my future had no real meaning unless I was in school, and I wanted to return. The person who really got me back in school was my uncle. He literally dragged me from school to school trying to get me in. We went to three schools in the same day—and we were walking. I had blisters on my feet by the time I got home.

"You're going to school whether you like it or not," he raved. "You wasted enough time. If no school will take you then you're going to your zone and that's final!" The next day I was enrolled.

When I returned, I already had it in my mind that I was going to pass all of my classes and be on the honor roll and return to the kind of student I used to be. But that only lasted one quarter of the semester. I was so used to not being in school that it was hard for me to get used to the class rules and get focused. I started out my days saying that I was going to succeed—but I found I was behind more than I had expected.

I constantly felt like I was under water and needed some air to breathe. "How am I going to catch up?" I wondered. What made it harder was that I was also trying to prove myself to people in my family. See, in my family, there aren't many graduates. My mom never made it past 9th grade and she repeated it three times. My uncle Luis made it to Long Island University but never completed his course of study. Still, he, my mom and my grandma instill in me the desire for an education.

But other people in my family, like my aunt Lucy, fill me with doubt. She tells me I'm too high up on my horse and soon I'm going to fall off, and sometimes that negative talk makes it easier for me to fall.

I always said I wasn't going to be like my family, I was going to make it, but when I found school hard and began to mess up, I found

myself thinking, "Oh my God, maybe I am nothing and am destined to be nothing," and that scared me. Besides, it was easy to cut. All my friends were cutting, too.

It would be "Come on Diana—let's go chill. Come on—after today you could stop but just for today let's go do something. Come on it's only the beginning of the term—these first few days of classes don't really matter, you could make it up later," and so I was pulled in. And at my school, anyone wanting to leave the building could just walk right on out past security.

They don't care what happens to us once we go out those doors, and actually, I don't blame them—we make our choices for ourselves. If we want to learn, we go to school—if we don't, we become no shows. Which is what I became.

By January, I found myself cutting more and more by myself. After a while, I would only show up for two or three periods (mainly so my twin wouldn't tell my grandmother, who I was living with then), and then I would leave. Usually I would cut at least one full day of classes each week. Instead, I would just hang around, explore Sears and chill at Mickey D's when it got chilly.

All that time, I didn't really see the future past the next day or week or month, and I assumed I had all the time in the world to correct my mistakes. The only time I thought about the future was when I was daydreaming. I would daydream about my senior prom and my graduation, with my whole family there clapping and cheering, some crying that I actually made it.

But sometimes I'd blink and I'd be back to the present and it was "Oh Wow! I have a lot to accomplish and so little time to do it." And if you're like me, this is usually the time where you get stuck and shake your head like a wet dog shakes his body and say to yourself, "What am I going to do?"

But after I pulled my hair out a little, I would get laid back and tell myself, "Oh, well, no one's perfect." I would convince myself that my family couldn't be mad at me because they didn't make it anywhere themselves.

At the end of the year, when I got my final report card, I realized I only had seven credits for the whole year. I laughed at this, but I also decided again that next year I would do better. But I didn't. By November, I was already messing up. I would go to school feeling that this time I was going to make it, then things would appear harder than they really were. I would get frustrated and search for an escape.

In February, I decided to enroll in a class to get my GED in order to not have to go through the stressing ordeal of high school. But I was bored, and after about three weeks, I dropped that, too. I worked full-time at a store, and when I wasn't at work I was lying down watching TV. Sometimes I watched talk shows from 11 a.m. until 5 p.m. I was very lazy, tired all the time. I gained a lot of weight and felt worse and worse about myself.

Then I got even more depressed, quit my job and was stressed most of the day. I was your average couch potato. During the spring and through the summer, all I remember thinking was "Damn, now I have no job, no money and no school to keep me busy."

This time I was of age to work, but I couldn't find a job. But in May I heard about City-As-School, and I decided to apply. It's an alternative high school and you work in the business world for your school credits.

> **I'm still struggling. I still have doubts.**

Now that I'm in school, for the most part I enjoy it. Sometimes I get a little hectic and those old feelings come back to haunt me. Like today, I went to school to discuss when I'll be graduating. I looked at my transcript and I needed so many credits. I thought, "I'm never going to make it." But you know what, this time I'm going to try to take things at my own steady pace.

I still don't have my act completely together. I'm still struggling. I still have doubts. When I mess up, it's kind of like a tornado—it swirls and swirls and it doesn't end until it's done with all of its destruction. Then, I pick up the pieces and start over, because the worst has already happened. All that's left is the endless effort to fix and correct. Still, I get sad and mad at myself because this is not what I want to be doing

with myself.

I guess I'm beginning to think of my life like that old folktale "The Turtle and the Hare." The hare was always looking for the shortcuts, sure he was going to win the race. The turtle took his time.

The hare relaxed. He napped. But soon he awoke and realized the turtle was inches from winning the race. The hare became hectic and tried to rush, but the turtle reached the finish line first, and the hare lost.

I was that silly rabbit—but slowly I'm becoming that turtle. I will make it and reach my finish line. I won't give up. I'm going to graduate no matter what. I'm going to stay in school and not only prove myself to my family but prove myself to myself.

WHAT I LEARNED FROM ROBERTO CLEMENTE: LATINOS NEED TO STAY IN THE GAME

By Luis Reyes

When I was 12 years old, I played for a baseball team called Puerto Rico. And what a hard and unhappy season I had.

I had practiced very hard, and at first I was hot. In my first five games, I hit six home runs and 14 RBIs (runs batted in). Everyone thought that we were going to be a championship team. But after the fifth game, I went into a terrible slump. In the next four games, I was one for 16. And in one game, I dropped an easy pop up that made us lose.

After that game, no one wanted to speak to me. The team was so mad that I got into a fight with one of my own teammates, who told me that I should go try out for Little League.

All those little words really hurt my feelings. And to make life worse, I was benched for the rest of the season. I was bristling. But in some ways, it was good that I was benched because I was too scared to go back out and play. I had lost all faith in myself.

One day after I argued with our pitcher, my coach told me to sit down and relax. Then he started telling me that I reminded him of a baseball legend named Roberto Clemente. "Who is Roberto Clemente?" I asked.

My coach told me that he was the first Puerto Rican star in the Major Leagues. He told me that there was a time when, like Jackie Robinson, Clemente was hated because of his race. But Clemente did not give up. My coach told me that Roberto Clemente was a man of heart.

When my coach told me this story, I went out to fish for more information. I went to the library and asked for old newspapers about his life and how he died.

I learned that, starting in the 1950s, Clemente played for the Pittsburgh Pirates for 15 seasons and helped lead them to two World Series. He also played in nine All-Star games, won the Most Valuable Player Award (MVP), four batting titles and 10 consecutive Gold Gloves. Amazing! On September 30, 1972, Clemente made his 3,000th career hit. Only 10 other players before him had made as many hits.

But his achievements came to a sudden end. On December 31, 1972, Clemente was killed in a plane crash while taking supplies to earthquake victims in Nicaragua. In 1973, Clemente became the first Puerto Rican player to be admitted to the Baseball Hall of Fame.

Clemente got to the Hall of Fame because he worked hard to get there.

When I talked to my father, he told me that Clemente was always the first player on the field to practice. He said that when Clemente was down he always found a way to come up. Learning about Roberto Clemente made me believe that even when I want to give up, I have to have patience and faith. Clemente made me believe that I should and could still achieve my dreams.

> **It's not the way you begin that counts, it's the way you finish.**

I haven't always believed that. The people around me aren't very successful. Besides, there haven't been that many people in my life who have supported me, and lots of people put me down.

My sister was the only person who did encourage me—she helped me with my homework, hugged me when I cried, and told me, "Luis, I believe in you." But she died from drugs that summer when I was 12.

But Clemente made me believe that if I work hard now, I can be somebody. Plus, knowing about Clemente made me see that Latino children could be as successful as any White, Chinese or Black person on this planet.

Before I learned about Clemente, I felt very embarrassed about being Puerto Rican because a lot of the Latinos I hang out with are not good influences.

Well, half of my friends want to succeed and want an education.

They are trying their best to do well in their classes and prepare for the future. But the other half are either in gangs, in jail, on the streets or on their death beds.

Like my former friend Edward, who is 18 years old and thinks he is all that. He is a high school dropout, but when I talked to him about changing his life around, he didn't want to hear it.

Another friend, Jose, is in a similar situation. He is 17. He dropped out of high school when he was in the 10th grade and joined a gang. He told me he joined it to help young Latinos from being pushed around.

I don't have anything against that. I just think that he should go back to school so he can help Latino children with his mind and heart, not with knives, guns and violence.

Sometimes I've almost slipped into the same rut my friends are in. But luckily I've had positive teachers who actually cared for me. Still, all the teachers who have influenced me are Black. Learning about Clemente made me realize that there are also Latinos out there who can be role models.

It also made me believe that my sister's spirit was still in me, and it gave me the strength to go outside with my friends every other day and run around the bases about 10 times. It gave me the will power to throw the ball from left field to home plate over and over. And it gave me the heart to stay outside and hit fast balls that my neighborhood friends would throw me.

Today most younger people don't know Clemente. But I think they should, because I bet anyone that if Roberto Clemente were alive today, young Latinos would not give up so quickly.

Clemente is my role model. If I had never learned about him, I would have given up a long time ago. It is because of him that I try to play with faith, confidence, power and belief. That's why in 1996, I had a much better season, and I won my league's World Series MVP.

Roberto Clemente made me believe that it's not the way you begin that counts, it's the way you finish. And my team and I finished number one in a powerful way.

IN THIS GAME...
THE RICH GET RICHER

By Melissa A. Oliver

Imagine being suddenly thrown into adult life; you are handed a piece of paper telling you your profession, how much money you make, how big your family is—your entire destiny.

Imagine having to pay all the bills and depend on no one but yourself. That's what happened to me when I played a game called Reap and Loss with a group of about 15 teenagers at a youth program in Brooklyn this summer. The piece of paper they gave me said that I lived in a neighborhood called Nottus, was single and had a child. I was a secretary and made $2,200 a month.

First we had to go to the bank or check cashing place and get our money. There were two different types—green for the people who lived in Nottus and yellow for everybody else. When we were done with that, we had to go around the room paying rent, buying clothes, shopping for food, paying for surprise expenses (fixing a broken TV, for example), and, if there was anything left over after all that, entertainment (vacations, movies, etc.). It wasn't hard for me to pay all of my bills on time, because I had the money. My only problem was deciding how much of a certain thing I wanted to buy. I knew I could afford it.

Like me, practically everyone from Nottus had money. Many owned land or had some type of business in a neighborhood called Cenbrook, where the people had nothing of their own. If the people there wanted to buy clothes, they had to shop at stores owned by people from Nottus who were ripping them off.

The people in Cenbrook couldn't open bank accounts simply because of where they lived. Even if they could get to the bank in Nottus, they didn't have enough money to keep the minimum monthly

balance. When they wanted to pay their bills, they went to a check cashing store where they had to pay a special fee that people with bank accounts don't get charged.

There were people in Cenbrook who couldn't pay their bills. They couldn't get loans from the bank either, because they had no credit. By the time it was all over, these people were flat broke. One girl was walking around asking, "Where's the welfare line? Where's the food-stamp line?"

When I watched the game played another time, a boy was yelling that he was naked by the end because he couldn't afford to buy clothes. "The amount of money I have isn't enough to live," another kid complained. During the discussion that followed, one girl said that she was a pizza delivery person who only made $700 a month, but every cent of that had to go for rent and her landlord wouldn't give a her cheaper apartment because of the number of people in her family.

Even though I was left with $745 after paying all my bills and expenses, a lot of other people only had $20 to hold them over until their next paycheck—sometimes less. There were some who couldn't afford to feed their children or put clothes on their backs. One girl became homeless because she didn't have enough to pay her rent.

> **Look around your neighborhood. How many of the people who own businesses actually live there?**

At the end of the game the teens in charge asked us to hold up our money. Some people didn't have any. Even though when we started out the people who lived in Nottus' money was all green. A lot of us now had yellow money as well. But the Cenbrook residents were only left with a fraction of the yellow money they started out with. Hmmm...

The point of Reap and Loss is to show how easily money can flow right out of the community where you live (in the case of these teens, "Cenbrook," or Central Brooklyn) without your even noticing it. Look around your neighborhood. How many of the people who own businesses actually live there? What they're probably doing is taking a lot

of the money that you pay them back to some other neighborhood with trees and grass, picket fences and families with 2.5 children and a dog. A place where no one is like you or me. That's what "Nottus" stands for. Not us, get it?

Playing Reap and Loss made me realize that this is one reason why poor neighborhoods stay poor, while rich ones keep getting more and more money and have better things than we have. After the game was over, the teenagers from the Financial Leadership for Youth (FLY) camp who were running it explained that one way to stop this from happening is to deposit your money in local "credit unions" where, unlike in a bank, the owners and the people with accounts all live, work or worship in the community. At a credit union, loans go toward helping the "members" buy homes and start their own businesses, so they can take back the community that belongs to them.

MOVIN' ON UP; I WON'T LET THE GHETTO HOLD ME BACK

By Hattie Rice

As a kid, I believed that I lived a regular life with a normal standard of living. The truth was, I was born in a homeless shelter in New Jersey and then moved on up to the East Side—to a rat-infested city-owned building inhabited mostly by the elderly.

Inside you had your common street pharmacist selling drugs to the elderly (they were not for arthritis) and a guy who threw his wife out the window for not buying cigarettes. The crazy part was that after she busted her ass, she ran right back upstairs to him.

One day I walked into the kitchen and saw a rat the size of a cat (I call it a crat). I'm still traumatized to this day. There were so many roaches our white wall looked black. Eventually, conditions became so bad that the floor started to cave in and the building got closed down.

By then I had figured out I was living in poverty. When my family got evicted, I had high expectations that we'd move to a more appropriate place to raise children.

My first reaction to our next apartment was, "At least it looks better and bigger—three rooms instead of two for my father, mother, brother and me." Then I took a look at my environment and realized: this was the ghetto.

The block had more than enough drug dealers (it's been featured in three rappers' videos, which is definitely not a good look). This time, instead of drug dealers selling to the elderly, the elderly were the drug dealers. They were known as OGs and that's who the young up and comers got their game from.

This was also where my mom progressed from an occasional crack user to a straight-up Whitney Houston kind of fiend. The drugs were

heavy all around us, from the corner store to the barbershop.

Our place was marked by special holes designed by the artist known as Mr. Rodent—with the assistance of his 20 or so kids. They marked our clothes, doors and even walls with their smelly signature. I woke up to a rat in the tub, one in the fish tank, or one chewing at my door to start my day. I thought the rats were normal because, being a sheltered child, I never got to see how life was on the other side of the fence. I didn't question it.

But when I was 14, I was placed in foster care, one of the best things that ever happened to me. I moved to a group home in a better neighborhood: St. Albans, Queens. This community was beautiful (although the hair braider up the block sold both weed and weave).

The streets were as clean as if somebody had licked them, and the neighbors were friendly as could be. On Halloween kids actually dressed up to receive candy. On Christmas, families decorated their front porches (hell, they had porches).

I vividly remember my brother's amazed expression when he came to visit. He had his mouth gaping wide enough to fit three pairs of Jay-Z's lips. My brother said it was the best neighborhood he'd ever seen.

Then my cousin shocked me. While everybody in my family was telling me to get out of foster care and come home, my cousin pulled me aside and said, "Look at this place and look at where we live. You would be an ass to come home."

Seeing that happy neighborhood pissed me off. How could I have grown up thinking every home has a large population of rats when other people lived in homes where the closest thing to a rat was a pet hamster?

It was painfully obvious to me that living in private houses and enjoying larger incomes gave the people of St. Albans a more positive outlook. Parents who are well-to-do don't have four kids and only $100 for food for a whole month, so they aren't as stressed and the kids are calmer, too.

Seeing how people lived in St. Albans had a profound effect on

me. I realized I was unsatisfied with my life and I progressed from being a girl too scared and withdrawn to go to school to being an A student determined to reach a high standard of living as an adult.

When I was little, teachers and classmates called me retarded and told me I wasn't capable of amounting to anything, so I had made it my goal to read many books and prove them wrong. Still, I'd never believed my life would be much better or different once I got to be an adult. I needed a picture of a better life to realize that my books could take me somewhere I wanted to go.

Unfortunately, six months after I came into care, I moved to another group home—one in the Bronx, positioned right next to the projects. One block above us was the Crips, and one below was the Bloods. This, of course, brought on gang violence and the shootings that sounded like fire crackers on the 4th of July.

I lived across from a park infested with rats the size of rottweilers (I call them ratweilers) and saw little kids on the street, no shoes, with just popcorn for dinner. I knew what their mom and pops were on. I know all about having to stand outside of churches, waiting and praying for a meal (and I don't even believe in God).

> **I needed a picture of a better life to realize that my books could take me somewhere I wanted to go.**

Every day I saw how the neighborhood affected kids' dreams. I asked one boy what he wanted to be in the future and he replied, "Nothing." I asked another, "What's your hobby?" He said, "Standing on the corner making money."

I understand why they're selling. The drug dealers are the ones with money, and if someone has a beautiful house, car and boyfriend or girlfriend, wouldn't you admire that person? The only problem is that, in the 'hood, the respected idol is a drug dealer, and people in the 'hood die over respect because they feel they have nothing else.

In theory, schools are supposed to help kids move beyond the life they know, but at my school, at least, that's not happening. Recently my guidance counselor showed me that the number of freshmen com-

ing into my high school is staggering compared to the low number of seniors who graduate.

Your environment molds your expectations. If you see everybody around you failing, you'll likely fail too, unless you fight like hell against it. If your dad and mom met while he was selling drugs and she was buying, it's more likely their baby will turn out to be a lookout for 5-0 than a Yale graduate.

But I believe that it's possible for me to block out everything around me and all the painful, negative things I've grown up with. I'm sure that if I stay focused and succeed in school, I can make it out of the ghetto.

Since I came into foster care, I've maintained my grades no matter what was happening in my life. And last year, when I got the chance to move to a foster home, I demanded to move to a good neighborhood and to live with a foster parent who could help me get into college.

> **Your environment molds your expectations.**

That foster home wasn't the greatest (I've moved yet again, to a foster mom who cares as much as I do about my college education). But at least it was in a nice area downtown, a serene environment with no gun shots and no kids screaming from a beating. I felt safe walking home because I didn't hear "Yo, Shorty!" on every corner or see a bunch of broke-ass hustlers. Instead I saw businessmen talking on their cell phones.

The neighborhood inspired me and I felt like I could calm down. Nights when I didn't feel like doing my homework I'd look outside and realize that one measly homework assignment wasn't going to keep me from my dream of being successful enough to live in a nice place as an adult. Of course, I also kept a 90 average.

In school, I'd often analyze what went wrong in some of the other kids' lives. In my new neighborhood, I had a chance to see how people went right.

Walking down the street I saw role models—business people on their way to work, heading into beautiful buildings. It was such a mov-

ing experience for me to walk among them, imagining myself one day working in one of those buildings or going into one of those homes, too.

TAKING BACK NEIGHBORHOOD PARKS

By Yohlanna Cort

You might recognize Open Road Park on East 12th St. from the 1996 movie *Joe's Apartment*. They show it in a scene at the end where the roaches build a garden. It looks like a tiny version of Prospect Park sandwiched between two buildings.

There's a garden in front with plants and fruit trees, a pond surrounded by birds and butterflies, a field in the back, a playground and basketball court. But that beautiful place wasn't really made by roaches, or even by Hollywood. It was designed by two New York City teens.

Fifteen years ago you wouldn't have recognized Open Road Park. Back then it was a bus depot, before it caught fire and was left vacant for 10 years. Nando Rodriguez, the 26-year-old director of Open Road Park, remembers people selling drugs in the lot and homeless people sleeping there.

But in 1990, former teacher Paula Hewitt started Open Road of New York, a nonprofit organization that works with young people on environmental projects. She helped get the city to give Open Road permission to turn some of the land into a park. Nando and his friend Ralphie Santiago, then sophomores at Eastside HS next door to the lot, led the park's design.

"They loved what we did," Nando said, and the Board of Education gave them more land. By 11th grade, Ralphie and Nando had turned the entire vacant lot into the park I visited this summer.

This summer, the teens of Open Road took their interest in improving their community a step further. Open Road took part in a program called "Growing Up in Cities," which was created by the United Nations in 1970 to give young people a chance to make their neighbor-

hoods better.

Teen "youth leaders" interview neighborhood kids to find out what they think the community needs most and how they feel about where they live. Then they come up with a project to improve the neighborhood, and are given a $1500 budget to complete the project.

It's been done in cities around the world, from South Africa to South America, and in New York City, in Manhattan, Queens, Brooklyn, and the Bronx.

Open Road youth leaders interviewed kids around Manhattan's Lower East Side about their concerns. "Everyone had a problem with litter and the lack of safety," said Bianca Hendricks, 15, of New Design HS, who wrote the proposal to get funding for Growing Up in Cities.

She was surprised that even kids as young as 10 were aware of and concerned about their safety, especially in teen hang-out spots like Avenue D and Tompkins Square Park.

Like many people, I sometimes forget that you can make a difference at any age.

The youth leaders decided these areas could be made safer for young people, by holding block parties on Avenue D, for example, or by getting teen bands to perform in Tompkins Square Park. As for litter, the youth leaders have already started picking up trash and repainting garbage cans in the parks.

They've also taken note of the particular problems in each park—broken benches, torn volleyball nets and a lack of activities for teens. Next, they plan to discuss their ideas for fixing up each neighborhood park with the Parks Department, and to offer their help.

They've already talked to the neighborhood's Parks Department supervisor about Seward Park. They pointed out that the park has an open space in the back that's sitting empty, even though it's large enough for three basketball courts, a picnic area or even a performance

stage.

Though there's no money to redesign the park at the moment, the Parks Department told the teens they could submit their design ideas and possibly help with the process if the money does come through.

I n the meantime, the youth leaders have started a "Prove It With Improvement" campaign, challenging community members and representatives to improve the parks. The teens plan to write grants and create t-shirts and stickers to sell, raising money so that teens can be hired to clean up the parks.

Youth leader Sharif James, 16, of New Design HS, said one thing stood out during the interviews. When he asked kids, "Do you think you can make a difference in your community?" many of them said, "No." And while they're right that young people can't solve every problem, the teens at Open Road showed that we can do something.

Like many people, I sometimes forget that you can make a difference at any age. But the teens at Open Road showed me that, just like the roaches in *Joe's Apartment*, amazing things can come from the most unexpected sources.

To get involved with Open Road of New York or their
"Prove It With Improvement" campaign check out their website:
www.openroadny.org

RISING UP AGAINST POLLUTERS

By Patricia Rogers

When Dyhalma Anaya was 16, she walked into the UPROSE office on a mission. She went straight to the community organization's executive director, Elizabeth Yeampierre, and told her, "Elizabeth, I want to change the world."

Six years later, as an UPROSE (United Puerto Rican Organization of Sunset Park) youth organizer, Dyhalma has helped fight off a power plant the city wanted to build in her neighborhood, pushed for a new park where now there's fenced-off garbage, and is now taking on guys' harassment of girls on the streets.

Founded in 1966, UPROSE, in Sunset Park, Brooklyn, tackles youth justice issues in the community like police brutality, racism, sexual harassment, teens dropping out of school and pollution.

Pollution is a big problem in the neighborhood. The Gowanus Expressway runs through Sunset Park on an elevated highway above 3rd Ave. The 200,000 cars and up to 25,000 trucks that use the highway each day give off a lot of diesel exhaust.

Garbage trucks also spew their diesel exhaust as they line up outside the waste-transfer station in Sunset Park to drop off the city's garbage. There the garbage is made more compact before being shipped out of the city in other garbage trucks.

All that diesel exhaust is dangerous for asthma sufferers, since it can cause or make asthma worse. The three power plants within 10 blocks in the neighborhood don't help either, since they release pollutants into the air too. In fact, the area around 3rd and 4th Avenue in Sunset Park has one of the highest asthma rates in Brooklyn.

Murad "Moe" Awawdeh, 18, joined UPROSE six years ago because he and most of his family suffer from asthma, and he wanted to do something about it. He and other UPROSE youth organizers

127

fought hard to keep a new power plant from being built on the neighborhood's waterfront.

They made a short film about pollution in their neighborhood, called Industrial Takeover, which was shown at the United Nations. They alerted community residents by blanketing Sunset Park with fliers, organized rallies and met with elected officials. They argued that power plants should be built in the neighborhoods that use them, not just stuck in poor neighborhoods, as they often are. And they won! Fighting to keep his neighborhood free from more pollutants "gets me all hyped up," said Moe.

The day I visited UPROSE, Moe was preparing to go to a meeting for the Organization of Waterfront Neighborhoods, which is working to make the waterfront cleaner and more accessible to neighborhood residents. With Sunset Park's power plants and waste-transfer station next to the river, "we have a waterfront that no one can go to," Moe explained. He's trying to change that by keeping out polluting industries and having parks built instead.

Other UPROSE members were about to go door to door to raise awareness for their Urban Forestry Project, where they explain to neighborhood residents how they can get a free tree from the city for their block. UPROSE hopes to get Sunset Park's streets lined with trees to make the air around the highway cleaner and to create shade to help keep cooling costs down. They're also leading community members in designing a nature trail that will connect Sunset Park to Red Hook and Bay Ridge.

As they walked out of the building with Dyhalma leading them in her cut-off red UPROSE shirt, they looked like a family ready to go fight for what was right.

For more information on UPROSE, visit www.uprose.org.

WASHINGTON HEIGHTS IS THE BOMB: TEENS WORK FOR THEIR 'HOOD

By Marilyn Urena

One day last fall at 6:45 a.m. at the 168th Street station in Washington Heights, 15-year-old Emmanuel Diaz (not his real name) was waiting for the train to go to school. A stranger not much older than himself came up to him and said, "How you doing? You look kinda young. You don't wanna die, right?"

"I looked at him like he was dumb. Then he was like, 'Well, I got this gun right here—you see?' He sat the gun on his lap," Emmanuel said.

The mugger took Emmanuel beeper and $5. "I was kinda scared, but I wasn't so scared that I didn't want to go to school the next day. I said to myself, 'Well, it happens to the best of them,'" Emmanuel said.

But being mugged made Emmanuel want to dedicate more time to helping other kids in Washington Heights improve the neighborhood. He decided to put in more hours at a community service program called Fresh Youth Initiatives (FYI), where he was already a member.

"Washington Heights is a good, safe place even though there are still some criminals. I don't see why we should let them ruin our community," he said.

Usually, when people hear the name Washington Heights, they seem to think about poor people, drugs and the zoned school. Some of this is true, but it's not all bad, and it's gotten a lot better in recent years. The neighborhood is improving, and youth are contributing to the change by volunteering at daycare centers, helping the homeless and doing other community service.

High school students tutor children at the YMCA, and there are places like the Armory where youth can just do something fun or cre-

ative after school, like play basketball, instead of being on the streets. Alianza Dominicana also has programs especially for Dominican youth.

FYI is an activist organization founded in 1994 that encourages the young people of Washington Heights to help the community. It was started because "young people weren't being asked to take part in the community," said Tanya Ortiz, the program director at FYI.

Today FYI has nearly 200 members, and 20 youth do community service projects daily. Youth from about 10 to 19 years old can become members. They simply fill out applications and they're in. Then, if they go every day, they can get homework help in the FYI office, and do community service from 4 to 6.

They have different community service activities, such as cleaning parks, painting murals, making sleeping bags for the homeless, tutoring younger kids, and working in the Helping Hands food bank, which is operated entirely by FYI. When I walked inside the FYI office, everyone was buzzing around, busy doing something. "We're always busy," said Lindell Palmer, 15, a student at Vanguard HS. "FYI shows you how to be responsible."

One wall of the office had FYI members' names with a weekly update of the number of community service hours each person had done in the week. The hallway was decorated with newsletters, pictures of FYI youth on trips, and newspaper and magazine articles about FYI.

I was pretty impressed. I thought, "Boy, these people must work hard because they sure do draw attention to themselves." It was interesting to me that in Washington Heights, which has such a bad reputation, there was a youth organization with such a positive mission for the community.

The community activity attracts a lot of members. "I saw some FYI members painting in the park one day and I joined in because I love to draw," said Lindell. "They told me about FYI and after painting, I asked how I could join."

Lindell explained why FYI works, saying, "FYI not only gives

kids a chance to better their community, it lets them do it together and rewards them for it. The rewards give the youth motivation to keep on going; it's something to look forward to at the end of a hard day of work."

Depending on how many hours of community service they gave, the youth of FYI receive gifts such as concert tickets (two lucky FYI girls got to meet the Backstreet Boys!) or hats, bags and shirts. The group also rewards the most committed members with out-of-state trips every year, like one recently to northern California.

But FYI isn't just about the material rewards. "FYI has helped me as a person," said Lindell. "It has helped me emotionally and physically. Emotionally, I see and can sympathize with people of lesser fortune. I can see that I am not the only person with problems or worries."

And FYI members also get a good workout. "It's a killer on the back," said Lindell. "Canned food is heavy when there's tons of it."

At Helping Hands food bank, "you stack shelves, talk to your friends, sing or dance," said Amaris Taveras, a 12-year-old FYI member who attends IS 90. Amaris said she started there two and a half years ago when FYI visited her school and spoke to her class about the trips they took, the new people they met and the community service.

On her first day, Amaris said she was "shy and nervous. At first I hung around with my friend. Then I met other people and I wasn't shy anymore."

Now, Amaris is at FYI every day by 3 or 4 p.m. and stays till 6, or 7 if there's a special event. "FYI made the community better and prettier," said Amaris. "Every year we have a serve-a-thon and block parties on my block. Before FYI, there wasn't anything."

Teens who volunteer at FYI have become proud of living in their neighborhood. "Washington Heights is the bomb! It's like being in Times Square but uptown—because it's always live," said Lindell. "And FYI makes Washington Heights better because it gives the youth a chance to do something for their community."

STICKING UP FOR BUSHWICK: YOUTH RALLY FOR MORE SUPPORT

By Roxana Monge

It was cold, but that didn't stop the teens from standing outside in T-shirts that said Make the Road by Walking, (Se Hace el Camino al Andar). It didn't stop the little children from dancing, either.

Lots of people also held posters that said, "We need more youth programs NOW!" The cars slowed on Knickerbocker Avenue to watch. Meanwhile, youth organizers attempted to fix the speakers and microphone.

Then Julissa Gonzalez, 17, began the protest without a mike. "Good evening everyone!" she yelled. "I want to welcome you all to Youthstock '99." Julissa and 40 other youth were holding a rally in front of the office of City Council member Martin Malave-Dilan. They were there to request that he fund a performing arts center and a homeless teen center.

Even though there was no sign of hostility, police barricades and officers surrounded the group during the rally. The rally was organized by Julissa and other members of a new youth group at Make the Road by Walking, a non-profit organization focusing on welfare, environmental, workplace and youth issues in the Bushwick neighborhood of Brooklyn.

Julissa and a small group of other teens set up the youth group, called Community Action Learning Project, about four months ago, for teens who wanted to do something positive with their time and also make their community a better place. The group meets on Wednesdays and Thursdays from 4 to 7.

Bushwick is mostly Puerto Rican and Dominican. More than half of the population there is under 18. The community is extremely

poor. Young people there are "in dire need of services," said Oona Chatterjee, a director of Make the Road by Walking.

The members of the Community Action Learning Project know the problems of Bushwick—they grew up there—and they're making change in small ways. One of the things they did was make a directory of the youth services in the neighborhood.

That's when they found out that in Bushwick, there are about 40,000 youth between the ages of 10 and 24 but only 2,000 slots available for them in teen programs. This is obviously not enough. This motivated them to demand more youth services.

Julissa, an outgoing and active Puerto Rican who has lived in Bushwick for 16 years, thinks the youth of Bushwick would be more likely to do something positive with themselves if they had more support. "I see that a lot of youths don't have anywhere to go when they have a problem. They need help and need a place to go to get it," Julissa said.

These teens feel that Bushwick needs a homeless teens program because there are many teens in Bushwick with nowhere to go. "There are homeless shelters but they are for adults and families. None of them give services that teens need," like youth-directed counseling services and legal aid, Julissa said.

Franklin Vidal, a Community Action Learning Project member, said that a friend of his had left an "unstable" home and ended up homeless. "It is unfortunate that this person could not participate in a homeless teen program," he said.

They also want a performing arts center where young people could go to develop their talents, since many of the young people in the Project are dancers. In the '60s, the Bushwick neighborhood helped pioneer "uprock," a dance of jerks and burns that evolved into break-dancing.

The group decided to have a rally, in front of their council member's office as a way to get the whole community involved and to show the council member that the community is concerned. They also planned to perform to demonstrate that they have talents and need a

performing arts center to develop them.

All city council members have what are called "discretionary funds," money they can use to fund projects of their choice in their neighborhoods. The young people were hoping Malave-Dilan would give them the support to start new programs. They faxed him an invitation to attend the rally.

After they sent the fax, Make the Road by Walking called the council member's office to ask if it had arrived, and his secretary confirmed that it had. "Even on the day of the protest we called his office to see if he was going to attend," Oona said, "and the secretary told us that he might make it."

But when asked about it later in an interview, Malave-Dilan said that he didn't attend the rally because he wasn't aware of it.

At the rally, the young members shared their experiences of growing up in Bushwick. "There are young kids out here (in Bushwick) going to jail. They are killing each other every day and I think that if we can get these programs out here in Bushwick, there will be less kids out in the street," said Yari Mercado.

> It can be a frustrating effort, but these young people are sticking with it.

After the rally, Julissa called the council member's office and was able to set up a meeting with him. Ten teens and two adult members of Make the Road by Walking told Malave-Dilan their needs, but they weren't able to reach an agreement.

Earlier, Malave-Dilan told me that "Bushwick is a community that has more than its fair share." He also said he "will not support any more homeless shelters." But when he was talking to the teens from Make the Road by Walking, Malave-Dilan told them that he wasn't sure if he would support their programs and that he wouldn't know until February. The youths left the meeting feeling rejected.

Still, they have hope, because even if their council member doesn't agree with all their requests, he is willing to meet with them and listen.

The teens at Make the Road by Walking have scheduled another meeting with Malave-Dilan and also with Council member Victor Robles to talk more about their plans. It can be a frustrating effort, but these young people are sticking with it. They are working together to bring about positive changes for the teenagers in Bushwick.

THE UNDERCOVER TEENS OF TOBACCO YOUTH

By Evelyn Gofman

"I'm a snitch, but hey! We get paid for it."

That's how Tyshawn, a 17-year-old from the Bronx, explains how others see his work for Tobacco Youth. By purchasing cigarettes, Tyshawn exposes cigarette vendors who break the law and sell to minors. Tobacco Youth, a program of the New York City Department of Consumer Affairs, started in 1998. There are currently about 35 teenagers working undercover.

Tyshawn and John, 17, of Manhattan, told me what their job involves. They start at "base" and drive to various locations throughout the five boroughs with their inspectors. The inspectors witness whether or not a purchase was made and head back to the car with the minor.

If a sale's made, the inspector will fine the vendor. "Once, I got a sale and the guy came out and started looking a few blocks around. He didn't see me but I saw him," John said. "He was mad; he wanted to find me."

The vendors may get a $1,000 to $2,000 fine depending on whether it's the first or second violation. Repeat offenders lose their licenses. "They deserve whatever they get, 'cause they shouldn't sell to minors in the first place," Tyshawn believes. "It's their duty to check ID."

It's important to keep cigarettes away from teenagers because most people start smoking in their teen years. And the younger a person is when she starts smoking, the harder it is for her to quit.

Tobacco Youth Coordinator Loida Arias said she smoked cigarettes as a teenager, too. "I started smoking just to be in the 'in' crowd and be part of the group and it ended up being a lot worse," she said. "If we started this program a few years back, a lot of teenagers would've stopped," she added.

"We see the stores we return to—they don't sell them. Young people used to go to stores and [easily] get cigarettes, but now they can't," Tyshawn said.

"I think we've helped the city," said John. "We help kids, and help them do something else with their time and clean up the air."

The city has tried other means of pushing people to quit the habit, like drastically raising the cigarette tax from $0.08 to $1.50. Now some brands may cost over seven bucks a pack. "I know a lot of teenagers are not going to like the price," said John. "It's more money out of their pocket." He said he thinks that'll get teens to smoke less.

Tyshawn said he didn't think the higher prices would push teen smokers to quit. But, he said, "My personal opinion is why would you spend money on something that can kill you?"

> **The younger a person is when she starts smoking, the harder it is for her to quit.**

TEEN ENVIRONMENTALISTS: A BREATH OF FRESH AIR

By Renu George

For New York City teens, there are no nearby whales to save, or rain forests where we can all link hands and protest the killing of trees. Most of us don't live near a beach that we can clean up, or even know how to plant a tree.

But there are other things we can do to show we care about our urban environment—there is litter to pick up, benches to paint, and vacant lots to clean. New York City residents also need to be informed about environmental hazards such as lead poisoning and the toxic fumes that come out of incinerators.

In August, I attended a conference on "Youth, Sustainability and Environmental Justice," hosted by the Environmental Justice Alliance (EJA). The EJA's primary purpose is to get young people involved in environmental problems in their neighborhoods. It's about "what you can do to shape up your community," said Jordan Tama, 20, of Williams College, who helped organize the conference. I met a number of teen activists there who are doing everything from organizing demonstrations to planting gardens.

Every Saturday, Vincent Chen, 17, of Bronx Science HS, and seven other teen members of Asian Americans for Equality (AAFE), clean up their Lower East Side neighborhood. They do everything from simply picking up litter to painting the benches and planting gardens in the little park at the corner of Pike and Allen streets. Before Vincent and his friends began their clean-up campaign, very few people would hang out there. Now, however, senior citizens are coming out to sit on the benches and enjoy AAFE's handiwork.

Vincent is also really concerned about air pollution. He feels that because of all the smog and car exhaust, New York City is not a good

place for teens to exercise or even hang out outdoors. Vincent thinks that cleaner gas is the solution, but he admits that it would be more expensive than the kinds we use now. The only way to get people to buy it, he said, would be if the government made laws requiring it.

So Vincent is focusing his efforts on a problem he can help solve—the amount of litter on the streets of his neighborhood.

Like Vincent, Shaun Whitehurst, 16, of Boys and Girls HS, was inspired to do something about the environment because of the litter around his way. He encountered "garbage on the streets everywhere and every day," in his neighborhood of Bed-Stuy, Brooklyn. When he was 15, Shaun "just decided one day" to join a local environmental organization called the Magnolia Tree Earth Center because, he thought, "It'll be good for your health. It'll be good for people around and the environment."

Through the Center, Shaun now does presentations on recycling and composting (saving natural materials like fruit and vegetable peels and using them as fertilizer instead of just throwing them in the garbage). When he started doing the presentations, "people said that they didn't recycle. I hope I sent them a message." He wants teens to start recycling, instead of throwing trash on the street.

Shaun is also very concerned about deforestation (the cutting down of forests). It seems like an odd thing for someone from an urban neighborhood like Bed-Stuy to worry about. But Shaun explained the negative effect that deforestation will have on our air quality and how hazardous it is to our health. "We have to breathe this," Shaun said. He can't replace the forests that have been destroyed but he has started a garden in his backyard, and plans to replicate it in his neighbor's backyard.

As Shaun continued to talk, I could barely believe that a teenager much like myself knew so much and was so concerned about the environment. It was a nice change from the "What, me worry?" attitude of many other teens I know.

Gloria Diaz, 17, of El Puente Academy for Peace and Justice, in Williamsburg, Brooklyn, worries about a bigger problem than litter-

ing. An incinerator-sized problem to be exact. Gloria's school is right near the site where New York City has long planned on building an incinerator that would be used to burn about 3,000 tons of garbage a day. The incinerator would also emit fumes that can be hazardous to breathe. The people of Williamsburg have been successfully protesting the construction of the incinerator for more than 10 years because if it gets built "we would all be, like, getting sick," Gloria said.

Gloria got involved in all of this when she was 13. She wanted to feel as though she had a say in what happened to her community. "I see protesting as a form of empowerment," she said. "We were like, 'No! This can't happen!' and we fought against it." Gloria feels that protesting is, in fact, a teen's greatest source of power.

She feels that Williamsburg is the target of what some people call "environmental racism." That's the practice of putting environmentally hazardous things (like incinerators) in low-income and minority communities.

> **They have decided to take action rather than just sit back and complain.**

The incinerator isn't the only environmental problem facing Williamsburg, Gloria said. There's also the reconstruction and repainting of the Williamsburg Bridge. The problem arises from the fact that they originally used paint with lead in it on the bridge. Now the old layers of paint are getting scraped off and scattered around the area. If a small child should eat the lead paint chips, it can make her sick, cause learning disabilities and may eventually cause brain damage.

Gloria doesn't think that enough has been done to protect residents of the neighborhood from lead poisoning and that this too is a form of discrimination. That is why, in addition to protesting, Gloria has also worked on educating people about lead poisoning. She hands out pamphlets about it to parents and helps do lead screening-testing kids to see if they have lead in their systems.

A prospective doctor, Sree Panda, 20, of City College, is also concerned about lead poisoning. She did an internship at the New York Public Interest Research Group (NYPIRG) this past summer in order

to learn more about it. She worked on setting up a database of information on lead poisoning (its dangers, where to get tested, organizations that are working on the problem) as well as trying to organize a Lead Poisoning Awareness Day in Chinatown.

Sree got interested in environmental issues when she took a course on ecology at City College. She thought, "Why not do some real work on it?" instead of just reading about it. That lead her to join NYPIRG.

Lead poisoning is not Sree's only concern. She thinks the air quality in New York City is "atrocious—heat, smog, pollution, it just weighs you down," she said. Sree is especially worried about the effects of the toxic fumes that blow out from incinerators—breathing that stuff is damaging to everyone, but especially to small children, who can develop learning disabilities, brain damage, and cancer, she said.

Unlike many of us, these four people and the others I met at the EJA conference, don't just shrug off the grime and pollution of New York City. They have decided to take action rather than just sit back and complain. Fortunately for the rest of us, their hard work and concern have made some of our neighborhoods better places to walk, play and yes, even breathe.

To get involved, contact:

New York City
Environmental Justice Alliance
115 W. 30th St., #110B
New York, NY 10001
212-239-8882
www.nyceja.org

Asian Americans for Equality
108 Norfolk St.
New York, NY 10002
212-979-8381
www.aafe.org

Magnolia Tree Earth Center
677 Lafayette Ave.
Brooklyn, NY 11216
718-387-2116

El Puente
211 South 4th St.
Brooklyn, NY 11211
718-387-0404
www.elpuente.us

NYPIRG
9 Murray St.
New York, NY 10007
212-349-6460
www.nypirg.org

THE YOUNG LORDS: REBELS WITH A CAUSE

By David Miranda

When I think about all the homelessness in the streets, the poverty, the drug use, the way poor people get treated worse than people who have money—the list goes on and on—it makes me wonder why no one seems to really care. Everybody is always talking about how racist society is, or how we have a double system of justice, but is anybody really doing anything about it? Groups that do try to take action usually don't end up lasting too long.

One such group was the Young Lords Party, an organization of Puerto Rican youth who actually went out and did things to help their communities in the late '60s and early '70s. The Young Lords started out as a gang in Chicago. Then they came in contact with the Black Panthers, a group of militant Black revolutionaries. Former Young Lord Ritchie Pérez says that the Panthers taught them that, "Instead of fighting each other we should be fighting the people hurting our community."

Their first big fight was with the New York City Sanitation Department. In 1969, poor communities (which are often the most crowded) were getting less garbage pickup services than the richer neighborhoods just a few blocks away.

The Young Lords started to clean up the streets of El Barrio in East Harlem. They went out on Sundays and swept up garbage and piled it on the corners so that the sanitation department could come and haul it away. "Look, we're gonna help you out," they told the city. "We're gonna sweep the streets and pile it up so that you could pick it up."

But the Sanitation Department wouldn't do their part and the Young Lords figured that unless they did something more drastic the garbage wasn't going anywhere. They took the garbage and put it in

the middle of 1st and 2nd Avenues and burned it. That stopped traffic and attracted attention to their cause. The Sanitation Department finally did come and pick up the garbage. In fact, they picked up the garbage for months afterwards. "Unless you push against the system they never pay attention to you," explained Pérez.

The Young Lords believed that the system was killing their people with bad hospitals, lousy schools, and unhealthy living conditions and decided to do something about it. When they saw that little kids often went to school hungry because they couldn't afford to eat breakfast, they started their own breakfast program.

"It wasn't easy to get up early in the morning to pick up the kids, walk them to school, and then feed them," said Pérez. "It took a lot of commitment...[but] we believed it was our responsibility to serve and protect our community."

The Lords also organized clothing drives, and pushed for bilingual education which didn't exist at the time, and for free, better health care for all people.

In 1970 the Young Lords set up tables in the lobby of the old Lincoln Hospital in the South Bronx and let people voice their complaints. They wrote down what they heard and sent it over to the hospital administrators, but got no response. So they took over the building, determined to give it back to the people. One of the things they wanted to do was start offering a drug treatment program. Fifteen percent of the population in the area which Lincoln Hospital served was addicted to heroin at that time but there were no services for them.

"People would come in with heart attacks, cuts, shock, whatever it was, and they'd die sometimes waiting in the emergency room," writes Gloria Gonzales in the Young Lords' book, *Palante*. "We decided it was time to move...About 100 people went to Lincoln and we took it over. We had gotten the support of the workers and the patients at Lincoln. At times we'd even have to stop some patients from just grabbing some doctor's throat, 'cause the patients had just had it with this hospital.

"While we were there we wanted to set up preventative programs,

a day care program, do anemia testing, TB testing, lead poisoning screening—all those programs that [were] not being done in the municipal hospitals. But we were only there for 24 hours, a little less... before we knew it the place was surrounded by police and we had to leave."

The system also made people of color believe that they had no history. Through the media they got the idea that they were criminals and would amount to nothing (sound familiar?). So the Young Lords set up "Liberation Schools" and ran classes to teach people Puerto Rican history. For a lot of the members it was the first time they ever learned about their own history.

> **The Young Lords were regular people just like you and me.**

"The best thing about being in the group was learning to be proud to be Puerto Rican," said Pérez, "learning about our people's history and contributions and the things that were done against us. I think that the Young Lords greatest contribution is that we made people proud to be Puerto Rican."

Mark Torres, a member of Fuerza Latina, a group of young people that is modeled after the Young Lords, said he was inspired by their boldness. "They were willing to do things that other so-called leaders weren't willing to do," he said. "It took a lot of love and commitment for them to put their lives on the line for our people."

But the Young Lords had a lot of problems within the organization which, according to Pérez, eventually pulled them apart.

At that time the FBI had a program called COINTELPRO to break up militant groups such as the Young Lords and Black Panthers from the inside. The FBI would put an undercover agent in the group to encourage conflict and suspicion and instigate fights among the members. Some people in the Black Panthers even killed each other. Pérez says the Young Lords were also a target of the FBI's program.

People often want other people to do for them what they should be doing themselves. The Young Lords were regular people just like you and me. Most of them were the children of immigrants and they were almost all teenagers—some as young as 14. The majority were poor and lived in ghettos like El Barrio, the South Bronx, and the Lower East Side. Some were high school drop-outs, others were college educated, but they all had one thing in common: they decided to stop talking and take action.

So next time you say, "Damn, I'm sick of seeing all these homeless people on the street," or "I hate the fact that in my neighborhood the streets are dirty," ask yourself what you plan to do about it. Are you just going to let it happen, or will you volunteer at a homeless shelter or organize a cleanup on your block? It's up to you. You can either be a part of the problem or a part of the solution.

"Learn from the past," advises Pérez. "Understand that you are the continuation of this history. Ten years from now what you do today will be the history we study."

CREDITS

The stories in this book originally appeared in the following publications by Youth Communication:

"Can't Afford to Follow: My Family is Important to Me," by Charlene George, *New Youth Connections*, March 2007

"The Crew from the Parking Lot," by Ferentz LaFargue, *New Youth Connections*, November 1992

"Losing My Friends to Weed," by Jamel Salter, *Represent*, January/February, 1994

"Why Is Your Best Friend Your Best Friend?" by Tina Li, *New Youth Connections*, November 1996

"Growing Up Nuyorican," by Jennifer Morales, *New Youth Connections*, November 1991

"Color Me Different," by Jamal Greene, *New Youth Connections*, September/October 1994

"From Extensions to Dreadlocks: Black Hair Is Beautiful," by Zenzilé Greene, *New Youth Connections*, April 1993

"At Home in the Projects," by Fabiola Duvalsaint, *New Youth Connections*, November 1997

"Growing Up in East Harlem" by Jeanette Melendez, *New Youth Connections*, December 1990

"Thomas Jefferson HS: A School Deals with Death," by Michael Quintyne, *New Youth Connections*, April 1992

"Brownsville: Finding Balance on My Block," by April Daley, *New Youth Connections*, March 2006

"The Lower East Side: Only the Faces Have Changed," by Jia Lu Yin, *New Youth Connections*, November 1992

"Candy Apples to Crack Vials: A Walk Through Coney Island," by Sheila Maldonado, *New Youth Connections*, September/October 1991

"The Making of a Ghetto," by Cheryl Davis, *New Youth Connections*, April 2000

"Why Are Girls So Mean?" by Anonymous, *New Youth Connections*, September/October 2005

"When Things Get Hectic," by Juan Azize, *New Youth Connections*, April 1994

"In Too Deep," by Phillip Hodge, *New Youth Connections*, March 2000

"His Sneakers, My Dreams," by Suzanne Joblonski, *New Youth Connections*, November 1990

"Revenge in the 'Hood: A Deadly Game," by Michelle Rodney, *New Youth Connections*, January/February 1995

"Snitches Get Stitches: Adults, Get Real," by Zainab Muhammad, *New Youth Connections*, April 1999

"Turning In a Killer" by Anonymous, *New Youth Connections*, May/June 1997

"Caught in the Act," by Rance Scully, *New Youth Connections*, May/June 1997

"A Day at the 63rd Precinct Station Changed My View of the Police," by Nicole Burrowes, *New Youth Connections*, September/October 1990

"My 'Hood Is Bad for My Health," by Pauline Gordon, *Represent*, January/February 2005

"Chew On This: How I Quit Fast Food...And Lived to Write About It," by Carmen Rios, *New Youth Connections*, May/June 2006

"Put Your Money Where Your Mouth Is: Teens Learn to Fight for Good Food," by Natelegé Whaley, *New Youth Connections*, December 2005

"Better Than Big Macs," by Natelegé Whaley, *New Youth Connections*, December 2005

"Fresh From the Farm," by Natelegé Whaley, *New Youth Connections*, December 2005

"Dropout Blues," by Diana Moreno, *New Youth Connections*, December 1998

"What I Learned from Roberto Clemente: Latinos Need to Stay in the Game," by Luis Reyes, *New Youth Connections*, April 1998

"In This Game: The Rich Get Richer," by Melissa Oliver, *New Youth Connections*, September/October 1997

"Movin' On Up: I Won't Let the Ghetto Hold Me Back," by Hattie Rice, *New Youth Connections*, December 2005

"Taking Back Neighborhood Parks," by Yohlanna Cort, *New Youth Connections*, September/October 2005

"Rising Up Against Polluters," by Patricia Rogers, *New Youth Connections*, September/October 2005

"Washington Heights Is the Bomb," by Marilyn Urena, *New Youth Connections*, January/February 2000

"Sticking Up for Bushwick," by Roxana Monge, *New Youth Connections*, January/February 2000

"The Undercover Teens of Tobacco Youth," by Evelyn Gofman, *New Youth Connections*, September/October 2002

"Teen Environmentalists: A Breath of Fresh Air," by Renu George, *New Youth Connections*, September/October 1996

"The Young Lords: Rebels with a Cause," by David Miranda, *New Youth Connections*, June 1993

ABOUT OUR PARTNERS

PUBLIC/PRIVATE VENTURES

2000 Market St. #600 • Philadelphia, PA 19103 • 215-557-4400
www.ppv.org

Public/Private Ventures is a national nonprofit organizaion whose mission is to improve the effectiveness of social policies, programs and community initiatives, especially as they affect youth and young adults. In carrying out this mission, P/PV works with philanthropies, the public and business sectors, and nonprofit organizations.

GROUNDWORK, INC.

595 Sutter Ave. • Brooklyn, NY 11207 • 718-346-2200
www.groundworkinc.org

Founded in early 2002, Groundwork provides a variety of services to children and families living in East New York, an economically challenged and physically isolated section of northeast Brooklyn. Groundwork aims to help young people and families living in or adjacent to public housing to develop their strengths, skills, talents and competencies through effective experiential learning and work programs.

HARLEM RBI

333 E. 100th St. • New York, NY 10029 • 212-722-1608
www.harlemrbi.org

Located in East Harlem, New York, Harlem RBI uses baseball and softball and the power of teams to provide inner-city youth with opportunities to Play, to Learn, and to Grow, inspiring them to recognize their potential and realize their dreams. Harlem RBI prides itself on being a community-based organization that successfully integrates youth development principles with the benefits of sports activity and team participation.

ABOUT YOUTH COMMUNICATION

Youth Communication, founded in 1980, is a nonprofit youth development program located in New York City whose mission is to teach writing, journalism, and leadership skills. The teenagers we train become writers for our websites and books and for two print magazines, *New Youth Connections*, a general-interest youth magazine, and *Represent*, a magazine by and for young people in foster care.

Each year, up to 100 young people participate in Youth Communication's school-year and summer journalism workshops where they work under the direction of full-time professional editors. Most are African American, Latino, or Asian, and many are recent immigrants. The opportunity to reach their peers with accurate portrayals of their lives and important self-help information motivates the young writers to create powerful stories.

Our goal is to run a strong youth development program in which teens produce high quality stories that inform and inspire their peers. Doing so requires us to be sensitive to the complicated lives and emotions of the teen participants while also providing an intellectually rigorous experience. We achieve that goal in the writing/teaching/editing relationship, which is the core of our program.

Our teaching and editorial process begins with discussions between adult editors and the teen staff. In those meetings, the teens and the editors work together to identify the most important issues in the teens' lives and to figure out how those issues can be turned into stories that will resonate with teen readers.

Once story topics are chosen, students begin the process of crafting their stories. For a personal story, that means revisiting events in one's past to understand their significance for the future. For a commentary, it means developing a logical and persuasive point of view. For a reported story, it means gathering information through research and interviews. Students look inward and outward as they try to make sense of their experiences and the world around them and find the points of intersection between personal and social concerns. That process can take a few weeks or a few months. Stories frequently go through ten or more drafts as students work under the guidance of their editors, the way any professional writer does.

Many of the students who walk through our doors have uneven skills, as a result of poor education, living under extremely stressful conditions, or coming from homes where English is a second language. Yet, to complete their stories, students must successfully perform a wide range of activities, including writing and rewriting, reading, discussion, reflection, research, interviewing, and typing. They must work as members of a team and they must accept individual responsibility. They learn to provide constructive criticism, and to accept it. They engage in explorations of truthfulness, fairness, and accuracy. They meet deadlines. They must develop the audacity to believe that they have something important to say and the humility to recognize that saying it well is not a process of instant gratification. Rather, it usually requires a long, hard struggle through many discussions and much rewriting.

It would be impossible to teach these skills and dispositions as separate, disconnected topics, like grammar, ethics, or assertiveness. However, we find that students make rapid progress when they are learning skills in the context of an inquiry that is personally significant to them and that will benefit their peers.

When teens publish their stories—in New Youth Connections and Represent, on the web, and in other publications—they reach tens of thousands of teen and adult readers. Teachers, counselors, social workers, and other adults circulate the stories to young people in their classes and out-of-school youth programs. Adults tell us that teens in their programs—including many who are ordinarily resistant to reading—clamor for the stories. Teen readers report that the stories give them information they can't get anywhere else, and inspire them to reflect on their lives and open lines of communication with adults.

Writers usually participate in our program for one semester, though some stay much longer. Years later, many of them report that working here was a turning point in their lives—that it helped them acquire the confidence and skills that they needed for success in college and careers. Scores of our graduates have overcome tremendous obstacles to become journalists, writers, and novelists. They include National Book Award finalist Edwidge Danticat, novelist Ernesto Quinonez, writer Veronica Chambers and New York Times reporter Rachel Swarns. Hundreds more are working in law, business, and other careers. Many are teachers, principals, and youth workers, and several have started nonprofit youth programs themselves and work as mentors—helping another generation of young people develop their skills and find their voices.

Youth Communication is a nonprofit educational corporaion. Contributions are gratefully accepted and are tax deductible to the fullest extent of the law.

To make a contribution, or for information about our publications and programs, including our catalog of over 100 books and curricula for hard-to-reach teens, see www.youthcomm.org

ACKNOWLEDGMENTS

This book is the result of a collaboration among many people at four organizations. It could not have been completed without their thoughtful and timely participation.

William Richards, senior education officer at Public/Private Ventures and director of the YET Program, and Helen Barahal, YET senior education officer in New York, helped to envision this project and played a key role in selecting the stories for the book. While she was at P/PV, Grace Cannon helped to demonstrate how Youth Communication's teen-written stories could be incorporated into the YET Program.

Trisha Williford, Nefertari Bey, Megan Demarkis and Luis Morales at Harlem RBI and Eric Haber, Erica Ahdoot, Furqan Khaldun, Katrina Huffman and the rest of the Groundwork Team helped develop the themes for the book.

This project was made possible through grants from The Pinkerton Foundation, The Clark Foundation and The Altman Foundation. Special thanks to Charles Hamilton and Marilyn Torres at the Clark Foundation, Nina Mogilnik at the Altman Foundation, and Joan Colello and Laurie Dien at The Pinkerton Foundation.

Thanks also to the leadership at each of the four organizations: Fred Davie and Leigh Hopkins at Public/Private Ventures, Rich Berlin and Rachel Cytron at Harlem RBI, Rich Buery at Groundwork, Inc. and Keith Hefner at Youth Communication.

Thanks to Tara Entwistle for proofreading and fact-checking this book.

Special thanks to the teens at Youth Communication for the time and talent they invested in sharing their stories.

MORE HELPFUL BOOKS
FROM YOUTH COMUNICATION

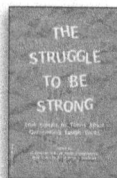

The Struggle to Be Strong: True Stories by Teens About Overcoming Tough Times. Foreword by Veronica Chambers. Help young people identify and build on their own strengths with 30 personal stories about resiliency. (Free Spirit)

Starting With "I": Personal Stories by Teenagers. "Who am I and who do I want to become?" Thirty-five stories examine this question through the lens of race, ethnicity, gender, sexuality, family, and more. Increase this book's value with the free Teacher's Guide, available from youth-comm.org. (Youth Communication)

Real Stories, Real Teens. Inspire teens to read and recognize their strengths with this collection of 26 true stories by teens. The young writers describe how they overcame significant challenges and stayed true to themselves. Also includes the first chapters from three novels in the Bluford Series. (Youth Communication)

The Courage to Be Yourself: True Stories by Teens About Cliques, Conflicts, and Overcoming Peer Pressure. In 26 first-person stories, teens write about their lives with searing honesty. These stories will inspire young readers to reflect on their own lives, work through their problems, and help them discover who they really are. (Free Spirit)

Out With It: Gay and Straight Teens Write About Homosexuality. Break stereotypes and provide support with this unflinching look at gay life from a teen's perspective. With a focus on urban youth, this book also includes several heterosexual teens' transformative experiences with gay peers. (Youth Communication)

Things Get Hectic: Teens Write About the Violence That Surrounds Them. Violence is commonplace in many teens' lives, be it bullying, gangs, dating, or family relationships. Hear the experiences of victims, perpetrators, and witnesses through more than 50 real-world stories. (Youth Communication)

From Dropout to Achiever: Teens Write About School. Help teens overcome the challenges of graduating, which may involve overcoming family problems, bouncing back from a bad semester, or even dropping out for a time. These teens show how they achieve academic success. (Youth Communication)

My Secret Addiction: Teens Write About Cutting. These true accounts of cutting, or self-mutilation, offer a window into the personal and family situations that lead to this secret habit, and show how teens can get the help they need. (Youth Communication)

Sticks and Stones: Teens Write About Bullying. Shed light on bullying, as told from the perspectives of the bully, the victim, and the witness. These stories show why bullying occurs, the harm it causes, and how it might be prevented. (Youth Communication)

Boys to Men: Teens Write About Becoming a Man. The young men in this book write about confronting the challenges of growing up. Their honesty and courage make them role models for teens who are bombarded with contradictory messages about what it means to be a man. (Youth Communication)

Through Thick and Thin: Teens Write About Obesity, Eating Disorders, and Self Image. Help teens who struggle with obesity, eating disorders, and body weight issues. These stories show the pressures teens face when they are confronted by unrealistic standards for physical appearance, and how emotions can affect the way we eat. (Youth Communication)

To order these and other books, go to:
www.youthcomm.org
or call 212-279-0708 x115

www.ingramcontent.com/pod-product-compliance
Lightning Source LLC
Chambersburg PA
CBHW070800290326
41931CB00011BA/2088